Thirty-four years have gone by since *The Best American Poetry* made its debut. The series now includes a total of thirty-six individual books. Every freelance writer must be something of an entrepreneur. The entrepreneur in me is proud of having articulated a vison, put it into words, refined the concept, persuaded a publisher to back it, and gone through all the stages culminating not just in one book but in a series of annual anthologies, year after year, one decade following another, across the century divide. My work as founder and series editor has enabled me to bear witness to what is happening in American poetry and to record my own observations in a sort of running commentary. —**DAVID LEHMAN**

PRAISE FOR DAVID L

THE BIRTH OF T

David Lehman's *The Birth of* The Best gives rea[illegible]-the-scenes look at the making of the yearly anthology he founded in 1988. Series editor of *The Best American Poetry*, Lehman has long had his pulse on contemporary poetry/poetries as well as the politics and culture that inform it. He has undoubtedly transformed and enlarged a readership for poetry. Luring many who might have otherwise eschewed it, he notes John Ashbery who once called poetry "our little secret." Or put more bluntly in the film *The Big Short*—"people fucking hate poetry." Censorship, social media, misinformation, the first amendment, editorial independence. Lehman has something to say about all these topics and more in his elegant prose. Prolific, iconoclast, and true believer, Lehman is the hardest working man in po-biz. And, like Frank O'Hara, Lehman knows that "Poetry, like virtue, is its own reward." —**DENISE DUHAMEL**

For over three decades, David Lehman has produced a compelling hybrid of literary journalism and poetic criticism characterized by prodigious urbanity, range, and timeliness. Nowhere is this more evident than in *The Birth of* The Best, which offers a fascinating glimpse into the process of his collaboration with guest editors of *The Best American Poetry* series and priceless reminiscences/appreciations of eminent poets. Lehman is especially astute in assessing the impact of cultural trends on poetry's subject matter, formal attributes, distribution, and reception. Perhaps the most crucial aspect of this essay collection is its thorough refutations of the ceaseless carping of those who would cremate poetry and dump its ashes into some musty attic, as well as those whose adherence to a particular orthodoxy would drastically limit its scope. Lehman is not an "apologist" for poetry; he is a vibrant advocate. —**THOMAS FINK**

THE BIRTH OF *THE BEST*

Also by David Lehman

•

POETRY

The Morning Line (2021)

Playlist (2019)

Poems in the Manner Of (2017)

New and Selected Poems (2013)

Yeshiva Boys (2009)

When a Woman Loves a Man (2005)

The Evening Sun (2002)

The Daily Mirror (2000)

Valentine Place (1996)

Operation Memory (1990)

An Alternative to Speech (1986)

PROSE

The Mysterious Romance of Murder (2022)

One Hundred Autobiographies (2019)

Sinatra's Century (2015)

The State of the Art: A Chronicle of American Poetry, 1988-2014

A Fine Romance: Jewish Songwriters, American Songs (2009)

The Last Avant-Garde (1998)

The Big Question (1995)

The Line Forms Here (1992)

Signs of the Times: Deconstruction and the Fall of Paul de Man (1991)

The Perfect Murder (1989)

EDITED BY DAVID LEHMAN

The Best American Poetry (annually since 1988)

Next Line, Please: Prompts to Inspire Poets and Writers (2018)

The Best American Erotic Poems (2008)

The Oxford Book of American Poetry (2006)

Great American Prose Poems (2003)

The KGB Bar Book of Poems (with Star Black) (2000)

Ecstatic Occasions, Expedient Forms (1987)

James Merrill: Essays in Criticism (with Charles Berger) (1983)

Beyond Amazement: New Essays on John Ashbery (1980)

THE BIRTH OF *THE BEST*

The Making of *The Best American Poetry*

David Lehman

MARSH HAWK PRESS · 2023
EAST ROCKAWAY, NEW YORK

FIRST EDITION
ISBN: 978-1-7326141-8-5
9781732614185

Every September since 1988 a new edition of *The Best American Poetry* appears, quickening pulses, provoking arguments. From one year to the next, the editor's name on the cover is different, as is the cover art. The series editor is the one constant: David Lehman. Here is the story of the development of this literary staple supplemented by the forewords he wrote for each edition since 2015.

Marsh Hawk Press books are published by Marsh Hawk Press, Inc.,
a not-for-profit corporation under section 501(c)3 United Stated Internal Revenue Code.

Cover and book design by Mark Melnick
Author photo by W. T. Pfefferle

LIBRARY OF CONGRESS CATALOGING-IN-PUBLICATION DATA
Names: Lehman, David, 1948- author.
Title: The birth of The best : on the genesis of an annual anthology / David Lehman.
Description: First edition. | East Rockaway : Marsh Hawk Press, Inc., 2023.
Identifiers: LCCN 2022054785 | ISBN 9781732614185 (paperback)
Subjects: LCSH: Best American poetry. | American poetry—Publishing—United States—History. | Anthologies—Publishing—United States—History. | American poetry—20th century—Periodicals. | American poetry—21st century—Periodicals. | American poetry—20th century—History and criticism. | American poetry—21st century—History and criticism.
Classification: LCC Z480.P63 L44 2023 | DDC 070.50973—dc23/eng/20230119
LC record available at https://lccn.loc.gov/2022054785

[clmp] NEW YORK STATE OF OPPORTUNITY | Council on the Arts

Publication of this title was made possible in part by a regrant awarded and administered by the Community of Literary Magazines and Presses (CLMP). CLMP's NYS regrant programs are made possible by the New York State Council on the Arts with the support of Governor Kathy Hochul and the New York State Legislature.

MHP Marsh Hawk Press
P.O. Box 206, East Rockaway, N.Y. 11518-0206
mheditor@marshhawkpress.org

for Glen Hartley

Contents

INTRODUCTION

The Birth of *The Best*

· 1 ·

Every September, a new edition of *The Best American Poetry* appears, quickening pulses, provoking arguments. From one year to the next, the editor's name on the cover is different, as is the cover art. The series editor is the one constant. It is the title I have held since the inaugural volume came out in 1988.

At bookstores and universities, or by digital means during and since the Covid pandemic, launch readings celebrate each new edition and let the public know which poems have gotten the nod from Sherman Alexie, Edward Hirsch, Natasha Trethewey, Dana Gioia, Major Jackson, Paisley Rekdal, Tracy K. Smith, and Matthew Zapruder, to name the successive guest editors since 2015. From 2003 through 2019, The New School for Social Research in New York City, where I taught in the graduate writing program, sponsored an annual gathering of the year's contributors in a crowded lecture hall with five hundred seats. On one such occasion, more than forty of the seventy-five contributors took part, some flying in from as far away as California and Greece. In the green room, the pre-reading excitement was palpable.[1]

As required reading in many college courses, *The Best American Poetry* is invariably on poetry best-seller lists—which may seem like an oxymoron but isn't quite—reflecting data compiled from independent bookstores. Inclusion in the book is a feather in a poet's cap; not being chosen is, well, how many poets do you know who feel they have won the recognition they deserve? As series editor, I am sometimes confronted aggressively: how come my poem wasn't chosen for *Best American Poetry*? I resist saying "maybe you didn't write one of the year's best poems" and explain for what seems the hundredth time that even a capacious book of seventy-five poems cannot accommodate all the fine verse and prose poetry published in any twelve-month period in a nation as large, diverse, and multitudinous as the United States.

People may suppose that the anthology is part of a literary establishment, an institution of long standing. On the contrary, it existed only as an idea and not a fully formed one when it occurred to me as I drove from Ithaca to the nearby hamlet of Ludlowville on the first Sunday in August 1987.

When Glen Hartley, my literary agent, submitted my proposal for *The Best American Poetry*, most publishing professionals thought that such a book as I had in mind would stand little chance of succeeding. Rejected by two publishers, both sympathetic but skeptical, *The Best American Poetry* became a reality only because an open-minded editor at a major trade house was able to suspend the industry-wide belief that books of poetry, good poetry, could not sell in sufficient quantity to make it worth the publisher's while. That editor was John Glusman, then with Scribner, which has been our publisher from the get-go. We have benefited greatly from the firm's editors, art directors, copy editors, proofreaders, and marketing personnel.

Every freelance writer has to be something of an entrepreneur. The entrepreneur in me is proud of having articulated a vison, put it into words, refined the concept, persuaded a publisher to back it, and gone through all the stages culminating not just in one book, but in a series of annual anthologies, year after year, one decade following another, across the century divide. Thirty-four years have gone by since *The Best American Poetry* made its debut. The 2022 volume reached me today (Sept 8, 2022), and I have three crowded bookshelves devoted to the series. Adding the two retrospective "Best of the Best" collections that appeared in 1998 and 2013, we now have published a total of thirty-six individual books.

My work as founder and series editor has enabled me to bear witness to what is happening in American poetry and to record my own observations in a sort of running commentary.

· 2 ·

At the same time that my BAP proposal was making the rounds in 1987, a renowned professor asked me whether I considered myself a critic or an editor first. A colleague of hers overheard and said, "He's a poet." Grateful for that recognition, I said that writing poetry was my reality, "an activity of the most august imagination," as Wallace Stevens defined "reality" in a late poem. Poetry is my base, but I never expected it to generate an income for me and I have always felt that writing prose and editing books and magazines were part of the deal.

I oppose the idea that one can be a specialist in one field only, or in one mode within that field. Why shouldn't we engage in as many interests as we had in college? I recall a year at Columbia during which I took courses in cinema, philosophy, modern British literature, Italian Renaissance painting, the English romantics, and the French symbolists. Why, then, need one limit oneself to one field of study or another? I have done a lot of different things: written poetry and nonfiction books, collaborated with artists and musicians, edited *The Oxford Book of American Poetry*, taught and lectured widely in the United States and abroad.

Nevertheless, I am glad the critic-or-editor question was raised if only because it prompted me to consider the relative importance to me of the various things I do. When put to it, I identify myself as a poet, an author, an editor, and a teacher in that order—by which I mean to imply that, for example, a poet wrote my books on Frank

Sinatra, American popular song, murder mysteries and noir movies. As a self-employed writer, I see editing and literary journalism as ways of teaching by another name and reaching, at least potentially, more readers than can fit in a lecture room.

By temperament, I feel more comfortable praising than scolding, including rather than leaving out. The critic gets to elucidate poems, books, songs, films, and paintings; to air enthusiasms that may prove infectious. The editor of an anthology gets to work on behalf of others and for the sake of the art form. Both sets of activities are well worth doing. The joy is grand when a piece of mine in *The Wall Street Journal* or *American Scholar* prompts readers to thank me for directing them to, say, George Herbert's "Love (III)" or Carol Reed's movie *Odd Man Out*. Equally grand is the joy of notifying a newcomer that her or his poem has been selected for *The Best American Poetry*—and hearing from them later that it changed their lives.

· 3 ·

The knowledge that *The Best American Poetry* has introduced and promoted worthy new talents that may otherwise have been overlooked is one thing that sustains the series editor and his associates through trying times. Poets who were well-known among the literati have gained fans in the wider world thanks to *The Best American Poetry*. Younger poets have entered the field. Terrance Hayes told me that the first book of poetry that he bought was the 1990 edition of the anthology, which Jorie Graham edited. Terrance added that he owned all the volumes in the series.

We have not stayed above the fray. On the contrary, we have caused controversies beyond the question of whether "the best" is a hopelessly subjective term or one that is valuable if the perspective is that of a distinguished poet, each year a different one, with the result that each volume can be construed as a response to the previous one. No poetry anthology will please all factions, but changing editors from one year to the next makes the impossible task of covering the waterfront a little more manageable.

Editing a ten-year retrospective in 1998, Harold Bloom chose to omit all poems from Adrienne Rich's 1996 volume. In his introductory essay, he mounted an attack on multiculturalism that met with a loud counterattack. In 2015, Sherman Alexie chose a poem published under an Asian name, but written by a Caucasian male who felt that the ruse enhanced his chances of getting published. This, too, caused an angry outcry, but we could always remind ourselves that our purpose is not to avoid controversy. Besides, we did not *perpetrate* the hoax; we *exposed* it by publishing not only the poem but the story behind it. After learning that "The Bees, the Flowers, Jesus, Ancient Tigers, Poseidon, Adam and Eve" was selected, Michael Derrick Hudson candidly revealed his method in his contributor's note: "After a poem of mine has been rejected a multitude of times under my real name, I put Yi-Fen's name on it and sent it out again." Sherman characterized the stunt as an attempt to "subvert what [Hudson] believes to be a politically correct poetry business." Why didn't he pull the poem? "Because it would have been dishonest," Alexie wrote.

It is my obligation and, it turns out, my great good fortune that I must write a foreword to each year's volume in the series. The Academy of American Poets has characterized these forewords as "state of the art" assessments. Nine of them inform the nine chapters of this book, each bearing as its title the year it represents and a pull quote from that year's column.

Written for the 2018 reissue of the first volume in the series, the first chapter gives an account of the birth of *The Best American Poetry* and is followed by the forewords I have written for the books that appeared in consecutive years from 2015 through 2022[2]—years marked by the Trump presidency, the Covid pandemic, the pollution of civic discourse by way of social media, new forms of censorship, and now Russia's invasion of the Ukraine. Naturally, these developments have had a profound effect on our poets and what they aim to do in their work. Threats to freedom of expression are scary, the deaths of major poets hurt, and the speed of technological change is rapidly accelerating and somewhat bewildering. The circumstances might not be propitious, but poetry continues to make its appeal as an art with a rich tradition and enduring vitality—an art capable of resisting conformity, asserting individuality, and providing a vehicle for celebration, lament, contemplation, vision, and the communion of self and soul.

CHAPTER ONE[3]

1988 Revisited: "Couldn't we just call it 'OK Poems of the Year'?"

When I conceived of *The Best American Poetry* as a series, it seemed to me that there were three indispensable elements in addition to the poems at the vital center of each book. We would need a distinguished poet to make the selections. An introduction by that poet and a foreword by the series editor would add value to the enterprise, as would a back-of-the-book comprising an honor list of the publications that were our sources and contributors' notes that went beyond the conventional.

For the debut collection, I felt that there was a fourth requirement: the year's guest editor would have to be John Ashbery. It is not that he was the only poet of great distinction and accomplishment. Nor was there the consensus around him that has emerged in the three decades since. Ashbery was, however, my own favorite and that of many friends and colleagues. He was effortlessly avant-garde, with a knack for puzzling even his growing number of admirers, and a history of arousing the notice of book-review editors and critics, including some who were implacably hostile to his work but interested nevertheless. I was curious, as I suspected many others would be, to know what poems he would pick to represent contemporary American poetry in 1988. The prospect of surveying the landscape with John Ashbery as our guide would, I thought, prove irresistible.

So it turned out to be. Multiple printings of the book were sold out before the official publication date of November 30, 1988. Copies were hard to find; the demand had exceeded the publisher's most optimistic expectations. I went into bookstores and learned that the anthology was sold out and on reorder. The book was destined to become a collector's item. In 1998, I walked into the greatly missed Gotham Book Mart, a jewel of a bookstore in New York City's Diamond District, with a cellar full of hard-to-find editions concealed from the public eye. The manager told me he didn't have a copy. He could add my name to a very long waiting list. "That was the first year they did that anthology," he confided.

The volume had to be done in a hurry. I had the idea for the series in August 1987. Two publishers turned down my proposal—one speedily, the other with reluctance. She liked the idea but couldn't rally enough in-house support for it. At the time I was a book critic by trade, and John Glusman, a Scribner editor whose taste I admired, was telling me about his spring list over cocktails. When John asked me what I was up to, I told him my idea and he said he would buy it. I thought maybe the martinis were doing the talking, but no, he made a serious offer, and we were off. Now all I needed to do was to persuade John Ashbery to take on the job.

So I phoned him. I loved phoning John because he liked to talk on the phone and was often more forthcoming during a haphazard phone call than at many a social gathering. I was nervous, because Ashbery was not always in favor of efforts to broaden the audience for poetry. In 1977, the poet Stephen Paul Miller, in an informal chat with John, asked him whether he had ideas for making poetry more popular. "No," he whispered. "Let's keep it our little secret."

Nevertheless, he agreed to serve as guest editor of *The Best American Poetry 1988*. I promptly sent him packets of poems that I photocopied at the periodicals room of the Cornell University library.

He procrastinated, as was his wont, and deadlines came and went. I phoned and he sounded plaintive. "Do I have to do it?" he asked with such pathos that I had to remind myself and him that he really did want to do this book. Luckily, John was, in the painter Fairfield Porter's phrase, "lazy but quick," and when he swung into action, he was decisive. He read through the poems I sent him, picked others from a wheelbarrow of journals and books, asked me to track down poems by poets whose work he liked and, before I knew it, we had a working list of seventy-five poems. John had decided that fifty, the number with which I started, wasn't large enough to accommodate the rich abundance of American poetry. He thought seventy-five would work better, and ever since, each volume of *The Best American Poetry* has had exactly that number.

The notification process that first year was homemade. I made typos and confused at least one contributor by saying that John had chosen "your poems" and then naming just one. John unhesitatingly chose Donald Hall's poem "Prophecy" from *The Paris Review*, even though he felt that the poem would be improved if one stanza were dropped. Naturally, I didn't mention this when I wrote to Don. But I didn't have to. When he sent me his bio note and comment, Don, an inveterate revisionist, included a new version of the poem minus the very stanza about which John had his qualms. Hall had arrived independently at the same conclusion.

Kenneth Koch, John's longtime friend and New York School confrere, responded to my request for a comment on his poem by saying: "I like the uncompromising title of the anthology." But like a number of subsequent guest editors, John had his reservations, particularly about the use of the word "best." He said, "Couldn't we just call it 'OK Poems of the Year'?"

. . .

As an editor, John expressed his taste enlarged by a live-and-let-live attitude that transcended schools, factions, and regions. I was impressed by his openness to poets outside his own supposed aesthetic range. When I characterized the contents of the volume as "eclectic," he corrected me, saying he had aimed to be "ecumenical." Here was an amalgamation of poets that would not ordinarily be found together in a single volume. Some were famous, or as famous as a poet gets to be, but we also had the voices of writers neither John nor I had ever heard of before we read their work in *New American Writing*, *Sulfur*, or *Shiny International*. Ten poets who went on to edit volumes in the *BAP* series were represented in the inaugural volume.

The book conjoined rebels, experimenters, and the academic establishment; eminences and newcomers; discursive poems and feats of wordplay. You had Ron Padgett, Michael Palmer, and Robert Pinsky back-to-back—and Ruth Stone, May Swenson, and James Tate. As for forms, there was a plethora. In "Farewell Performance," his elegy for his friend David Kalstone, James Merrill turns to syllabics, four-line stanzas with eleven syllables in each of the first three lines and five syllables in the fourth. In "An Old Story is Retold," John Hollander achieves an elegant lyricism in five a-b-b-a quatrains. Harry Mathews's sestina is a narrative tour de force built around "racism," "Fascism," "Marxism-Leninism," "sexism," "Maoism," and "militarism"—the poem's six repeating end-words, drained of their usual meaning. Lydia Tomkiw's strangely beautiful "Six of Ox Is" consists entirely of palindromes. Eileen Myles's "Public Television" would raise talk to a poetic ideal. There are poems in rhyme (Tom Disch, Anthony Hecht), a verse essay on language (Wanda Coleman), sonnets that break the rules (Ted Berrigan, Bernadette Mayer) and a sonnet that observes them (George Bradley), a funeral march, and a quintet of prose poems that made it plain that dynamic things were happening on that front. John constructed "American poetry" broadly, and three once-or-future Nobel Laureates, born elsewhere but resident here (Brodsky, Heaney, Walcott), made their way into these pages. We had Kenneth Koch on

Paris, James Schuyler on Mildred Bailey, Jorie Graham on difficulty, Donald Justice on nostalgia, Philip Levine on Tom Jefferson (a laborer, not the third president of the United States), and A. R. Ammons reminding us of "how the onset of time strikes at birth, how love falters, / how past the past is, how the eyes of hungry children feed the flies."

This was American poetry in 1988 as John Ashbery saw it.

. . .

In succeeding years, I turned to John for counsel on everything from cover art to the choice of guest editors and specific poems. John's own poems have been chosen by many editors of this series, a majority in fact, and our pages have been home to "Notes from the Air," "Baked Alaska," "Myrtle," "The Problem of Anxiety," "Wakefulness," "A Worldly Country," "They Knew What They Wanted," "Postlude and Prequel," "Breezeway," and "Commotion of the Birds," to name some.

John was sixty years old when he edited *The Best American Poetry*. He had just published *April Galleons*, his eleventh full-length book of poems. Still in his future were *Flow Chart* and fourteen other poetry collections; gatherings of his art criticism, his literary criticism, and his translations of French poetry and prose; the Charles Eliot Norton lectures he gave at his alma mater, Harvard; critically acclaimed collages that he exhibited at Tibor de Nagy Gallery; a host of medals, honors, prizes, and awards. On September 3, 2017, the unthinkable happened. John was ninety years old when he breathed his last.

In 2016, John asked me to pinch-hit for him at a reading of Pulitzer winners organized by the Poetry Society of America in the Great Hall of Cooper Union. From his prize-winning volume, *Self-Portrait in a Convex Mirror* (1975), I chose to read "Worsening Situation," because it was one of John's particular favorites. It was his practice when he gave a poetry reading to read only one or two poems from his most recent book, giving most of the time to new work. The poem from *Self-Portrait in a Convex Mirror* that John would choose to read when he gave readings in 1976 was invariably "Worsening Situation." With its constantly shifting surface, its wry humor, its rejuvenation of clichés ("everyone is along for the ride"), its subtle allusions to Keats and T. S. Eliot and its cheerful appropriation of the language of TV commercials, the poem is echt Ashbery.

Recently, Kevin Young asked me to pick a poem from the archives of *The New Yorker*. I would read it aloud and then Kevin and I would discuss my choice on a podcast. I selected "Worsening Situation," which I remember clipping from the magazine in January 1975. When I realized that I might be quizzed on the poem, I resorted to my habit of writing a poem "in the manner of" the poem at hand, and this homage to JA is the result:

On "Worsening Situation" by John Ashbery

Like a collage, I wrote, the bruised words
Shampoo the hair of the dog. Or like
The simile eclipsing the thing it is likened to,
Which remains unnamed. The feast is
Near enough to watch but too far to reach
By foot. To up the ante, we get an echo
Of Keats's last poem or a quote from Rimbaud.
The key repetition occurs here. We feel
We have been riding the A train since 1965.
Rides, ceremonies, rites. What's the point?
Yet it bothers me, everything I haven't disclosed
Fully. I still read spy novels and get crank
Phone calls. I'm like the guy whose wife
You see on TV wondering how to get
My collars clean. Tell her I'm somewhere
Else—Paris, Texas, for instance.

. . .

Working with John made you privy to his conversational brilliance and wit. Naturally, he talked about the poems we read and what he liked about the ones that made the final cut, but as a rule, John preferred talking about movies or the songs of Charles Trenet or what they're drinking in Paris these days ("le bourbon"). Exemplary and charming, his engagement with American popular culture informs his correspondence and will make an edition of his letters indispensable.

When, in an email exchange in 2015, I railed against certain overused terms (such as "issues," "procedure" in the medical context, and "narrative"), John replied, "Let's not forget 'scenario' (along with 'narrative'), 'customize,' 'eponymous' and 'rollout,' which I recently used in a title: 'Botched Rollout.'" Knowing that "Too Marvelous for Words" is one of my favorite songs, John volunteered that it was introduced in *Ready, Willing, and Able*, "a little-known Busby Berkeley movie of 1937 featuring Ruby Keeler but few of the other usual suspects. It's sung by Ruby, I think, while an actor named Lee Dixon tap dances an accompaniment on the keys of a giant typewriter. Check it out!"

In his next letter, John followed up: "I occasionally wonder about the career of Lee Dixon. It's impossible to find much on the web, except that he died at 38 in 1953, his 'career cut short by alcoholism.' The only other movie I know of him being in is the lackluster 'Gold Diggers of 1938,' at which point the franchise had pretty much run its course." As to his own health, and that of David Kermani, John wrote, "I still have my mobility issues and he's recovering from his hip procedure, but hey, what the heck, as Bobby Goldsborough wrote in 'Honey,' where it rhymes with 'She hugged my neck.'"

On my answering machine I had Johnny Mercer and the Pied Pipers singing the first notes of "Accentuate the Positive." The song goes on to command us to "eliminate the negative" and not to "mess with Mr. In-Between," but only the eponymous (!) injunction was on my machine. Modest as always, but always knowing, John prefaced his message with "this is Mr. In-Between."

CHAPTER TWO[4]

2015: "I'd rather die on my feet than live on my knees."

When you write an annual column for nearly three decades, you may, in effect, be writing a book in discontinuous increments. But you're not necessarily conscious of it. You don't consult the previous year's report before writing the present one, so when you put them together and reread the lot, you're likely to be in for a few surprises.

In 2015, the twenty-nine "Forewords" that had appeared to date in *The Best American Poetry* were gathered in *The State of the Art: A Chronicle of American Poetry, 1988-2014*, and published by the University of Pittsburgh Press. Rereading the pieces in consecutive order, I was struck not only by unconscious repetitions (Wordsworth on pleasure, and the formation of poetic taste, "abundance," as the defining trait of American poetry, W. H. Auden's observations, Oscar Wilde's paradoxes) but also, for example, by my evident partiality for the "not only / but also" rhetorical formula.

My pet peeves never let me down. I seem always to have been aghast at ad hoc pronouncements that pass for critical judgments and can rarely let it go unremarked when somebody lowers the limbo bar even in the act of elegizing some aspect of the poetry he despises. The December 2014 issue of the *Atlantic* provided a perfect illustration: a piece by James Parker lamenting, in the year of the Welsh poet's centenary, the loss of Dylan Thomas. The article's title states the theme: "The Last Rock-Star Poet."[5] As the last of that bardic breed, Thomas (Parker says) was worthy of our attention if not our unequivocal acclaim—except that as a poet he didn't amount to all that much. In Parker's words, "'Fern Hill' is gloop; 'Do Not Go Gentle into that Good Night' is inferior Yeats." That sentence, those judgments, are backed up by nothing. They are not even discussed, let alone substantiated, explained, argued. They are merely stated as if they were beyond dispute—articles of received wisdom elevated to self-evident propositions. I wondered whether the writer had taken the time to reread "Fern Hill" or was he merely, as was possible, revolted by the memory of a younger version of himself, who had a deep crush on Thomas, having been smitten, as he admits, by "the charm of the man, the charm of the boy, the shock-headed cherub-troll who'd come waddling down to London from Swansea with a cigarette between his lips and a brown beer bottle in his pocket."

"Fern Hill" is a full-throated evocation of Edenic innocence, a Romantic recollection of an enchanted boyhood in the tradition variously exemplified by Thomas Traherne in the latter half of the seventeenth century and Wordsworth a century later. I like quoting the last three lines of the poem because they reach for the highest notes available in bringing this elegy for youth to a close:

Oh as I was young and easy in the mercy of his means,
Time held me green and dying
Though I sang in my chains like the sea.

Is it possible that these lines make the *Atlantic* writer gag ("gloop") precisely because they are so rich and so affecting and because such qualities are as outmoded as neckties? The sheer passion of the writing; the artful repetition of key phrases introduced earlier ("young and easy," "Time" as a divine agent); the complexity of the final utterance, a subordinate clause that surpasses the main clause in its lyricism; the arresting simile at the very end—there is wizardry here, and wonderment, a sense of the natural sublime.

As for "Do Not Go Gentle into that Good Night," to dismiss Thomas's famous villanelle as "inferior Yeats" is a pedantry, and a false one. Use Yeats as your standard, and few poets shall 'scape whipping. But for the record, Yeats did not write villanelles, and the effects Thomas achieves in "Do Not Go Gentle" are not those that the Irish poet was after. In the face of his father's imminent demise, Thomas used the constrictive form dialectically, to discipline his feelings and to apply a restraint on his fountain of imagery and linguistic genius. The poem's second stanza attests to the power that he achieved through the use of the strict form:

Though wise men at their end know dark is right,
Because their words had forked no lightning they
Do not go gentle into that good night.

This is not a brand of poetry that would please the British poets of ironic understatement who chose Hardy as a master and whose greatest practitioner is Larkin. But it is a sterling example of Thomas's method, which (he wrote in a letter) was to let one image "breed another, let that image contradict the first, make, of the third image bred out of the other two together, a fourth contradictory image, and let them all, within my imposed formal limits, conflict." The method is at the service of something that can never stay out of fashion for long: the heroic note, defiance in the face of mortality.

Instant dismissal of greatness goes together with a second thing that reliably gets a rise out of me, the glorification of dumbness in American culture. A generously funded study indicates that there is a correlation between the elimination of course requirements and widespread ignorance of American history, civics, our government and economic structures. Although you might expect to see such a revelation in a satirical weekly, it gets half a page of a daily newspaper noted for its sobriety. Some readers may wonder whether we really need focus groups, task forces, or in this instance , a commissioned study to reveal what anecdotal evidence provides in abundance—or perhaps this academic exercise in stating the obvious itself lends credence to the argument. In any case, if you wanted the veneer of pseudo-scientific authority that only statistics can confer, you are now entitled to say that most college students do not know the length of a congressman's term, the meaning and purpose of the Emancipation Proclamation, or the name of the Revolutionary War general in charge of American forces at Yorktown.[6]

As if to signal its opposition to grade inflation—another villain in parables about the decline of an informed citizenry—the American Council of Trustees and Alumni has issued grades to universities and colleges. Both Wesleyan University, whose president has written in passionate defense of the humanities, and Brown University, that bastion of exclusive progressivism, were among the ninety-eight institutions that flunked. Fewer than one in five graduates of F-rated schools will have been required to take a class in American history. Even fewer will have been asked to study a foreign language or economics 101. As one who loved his Columbia education with its strong core requirements, it pains me that our graduates know less, and are expected to know less, than their counterparts in previous generations. It is as though the teaching profession has decided to abdicate its chief responsibility. But this I know: a lack of conviction in what you are teaching spells disaster. As Magdalena Kay writes: "Our current sense of crisis is partly a crisis of faith in what we are teaching, not just in how we are teaching it."[7] Kay quotes Christopher Lasch, prophet of the *Culture of Narcissism*: "When elders make no demands on the young, they make it almost impossible for the young to grow up."

Poetry may be the enchanted childhood, the "farm forever fled" in Dylan Thomas's ode to a lost paradise. But poetry is also an essential part of adulthood, and adulthood a more serious state of mind and being than an adolescence idealized by an eighteenth-century savant. I will continue to speak up for such allegedly outmoded things as canonical books, the study of Western culture and modern thought, the concept of genius, the value of the memorization and recital of verse, the sustaining power of the imagination, and the privileged status of the aesthetic considered apart from all political considerations. To an extent, I believe that the attachment to such cultural values puts one in opposition to the worship of handheld gadgetry. I will always favor the physical book, but it would be foolish to deny a changing actuality—and the benefits that come with it. While I don't find it natural to read, say, George Meredith's *Modern Love* online, I am glad this formerly hard-to-find sequence of poems is available there, and I believe, moreover, that it is useless to resist advances in technological efficiency. The medium may not be the message, but it alters the ground conditions of its being.

The idea of using social media as a channel for poetry has its attractions. Robert Wilson, editor of *The American Scholar*, initiated "Next Line, Please" on the magazine's website and asked me to serve as quiz-master and prompt-maker. Since we began the weekly challenges in May 2014, we crowdsourced a rhymed sonnet over the course of fifteen weeks; we then had competitions for best haiku, tanka, anagram, limerick, sestina, completion of a fragment by Emily Dickinson, opening and closing sentences of imaginary novels. Among my favorites was the one we devoted to couplets. Each entry had to have "fall" as an end-word, with the result that seven of the couplets, when combined, fulfilled the requirements of two forms—the ghazal and the sonnet, or what Mariam Zafar dubbed the "ghazal sonnet." Here's what we came up with:

> The better the book, the longer the farewell,
> the leaves in amber as their shadows fall.
>
> With a red gold fire raining down, we fall
> in love. The lonely branches sprawling tall,
>
> We lug the red-leaf-laden tarp like pall-
> bearers to curbs for trucks to haul away our fall.
>
> Of all sad leaves that curl and fall,
> the red are those I must recall.

My austral spring belies your boreal fall;
you burn brown leaves and dismiss my call.

On the yellow brick road to Damascus St. Paul took a fall,
as did Bogart in *To Have and Have Not* upon meeting Bacall.

Popeye chuckled and scratched his balls: on the wall
he scrawled, "Explore the mall in the reddening fall."

The authors were Bruce Bond, Katie Naoum, Leonard Kress, Lawrence Epstein, Diana (no last name given), Terence Winch, and John Tranter.

"Next Line, Please" was just one of several online verse initiatives that got started in 2014. *The New York Times* launched "News Verse" in December 2014. Poets were approached and asked to contribute a poem based on their reading of the day's newspaper. I was invited, and on Monday the 22nd, I wrote a poem based on the front-page article "Accusers and the Accused, Crossing Paths at Columbia University," by Ariel Kaminer. This well-researched piece about tensions on the campus of my alma mater made me ponder the conflicts revealed and the mysteries stated but unsolved.[8] Lifting whole phrases from the article, I wrote this:

Accusers and the Accused, Crossing Paths at Columbia

False reports of rape are rare.
The accused rapist, an architecture student from Germany, said
"My mother raised me as a feminist."
He supports equal rights for women.
Three women have accused him of "intimate partner violence."

One accuser takes a bed with her wherever she goes
Which doubles as her senior thesis
And, in October, students at more than 100 colleges
Carried a mattress or pillow to dramatize the crisis
Of sexual assault on campus.

The president said he favored "law and the principles of
    academic freedom
And at the same time protecting the rights of all."

The man in the watch cap sits on the steps of Low Library.
He said it didn't happen.
Most of his friends dropped him
Last year when Ms. Sulkowicz—
Or when the *Spectator* published his name.
Campus hearings have a lower burden of proof
Than criminal trials and he said he was not allowed.
But she did not press criminal charges.

None of them would ever get over it.

Though I did little more than rearrange choice parts of the article, making a few changes in wording and adding the final line, the editor in charge of "News Verse" informed me that the paper's "top editors along with the lawyers" decided against running the poem "given the sensitivities involved." The subject was too hot to handle in a poem. The decision surprised me, because my poem did not strike me as either particularly provocative or deliberately offensive. Maybe, I mused, the editors thought the poem was boring. But a wise friend countered that if it had been boring, the paper would have unhesitatingly posted it. No, I am afraid that the key words were "lawyers" and "sensitivities." The lesson, so far as I can see, is that what is acceptable in a fact-checked newspaper article becomes dangerous, or potentially dangerous, in a poem—even if the poem is absolutely faithful to the facts as reported. A poem is not a straightforward article; its meaning is not self-evident; it can be ambiguous, and if it is, it is dangerous, the more so at a time when the "sensitivities" of special-interest groups play a decisive part in limiting free speech on campus and everywhere else. From the newspaper's point of view, there was only a downside in posting my poem. They had wanted something harmless, or funny, or "poetic," not anything that could stir up emotions about such timely campus subjects as rape and sexual assault, "yes means yes" contracts preceding the consummation of an affair, the rights of the accused in rape cases, the effects on the accusers, the artwork as a substitute for a conventional "senior thesis," the way language reflects these tensions, the resort to platitudes by the university leadership.

I do not want to inflate the importance of my poem's fate. In journalism, these things happen all the time. But a larger problem bedevils us: the problem of censorship and self-censorship. In 2014, hackers purportedly on hire from North Korea made a cyber-raid on the electronic coffers of Sony Pictures. The hack attack was sparked by the studio's intention to release a broad comedy starring Seth Rogen and James Franco as a pair of journalists who are recruited to assassinate the leader of North Korea. It resulted in much egg in the face and a big hole in Sony's pocketbook. But the violation of Sony's cyberspace also delivered an unsubtle threat. Theater chains in the United States refused to book *The Interview*, not because it was a lousy film, but out of fear that some madman might bring an AK-47 to the mall and mow down customers. Sony withdrew the picture; President Obama rebuked Sony and promised to retaliate for the act of "cyber-vandalism," and the leader of North Korea labeled our president a "monkey." For a while, George Clooney couldn't get anywhere with a petition urging solidarity with the makers of the movie, and though the film was released in the end, if only in a limited way, what bothered fans of the First Amendment was how quickly and instinctively we and our institutions cave in to the demands of dictators, even those of the tin-pot variety.

The willingness to button up our lips does nothing to deter such shocking assaults on free expression as the homicidal attack on the editors, staff, and cartoonists of *Charlie Hebdo* in Paris on January 7, 2015. The satirical weekly that held nothing sacred, not even Charles de Gaulle, exists within a French tradition of caustic satire, brazen caricature, and principled impertinence. It has waged a war of wits with the forces of militant Islam. Back in November 2011, the magazine had had the unmitigated gall of mocking *sharia* [*charia* in French], religious rule based on ancient Muslim principles, unmodified by anything resembling a Reformation, an Enlightenment, or an Ecumenical Council. The cartoon on the cover of the issue entitled *Charia Hebdo* threatened "100 lashes if you don't die laughing!"[9] Five years earlier, the weekly reprinted the Danish cartoons of Mohammad that had aroused the ire of cutthroat jihadists. Surprisingly, many publications in America and abroad did not have the guts to do so. The editors of *Charlie Hebdo*, including the legendary figures known as "Charb" (Stephane Charbonnier) and "Cabu" (Jean Cabut), were among the twelve individuals killed in the attack of January 7. For the right to say what they thought, they paid with their lives.

On the very night that the Paris massacre dominated the newswaves, with Parisians in the streets holding up signs saying, "Je Suis Charlie," I heard a *New York Times* columnist go on CNN and tell newscaster Don Lemon that "We in journalism should try to avoid giving offense." It struck me as a very odd thing for him to say. Isn't giving offense, provoking discussion, stirring the pot, airing your views, part of the deal? A former press secretary to President Obama drew a distinction to the effect that while the press has the *right* to insult a religious leader, it may show bad *judgment* to wave a red flag in the eye of a stampeding bull. This is too half-hearted a defense of the freedom of speech and press, both of them under constant assault. In contrast, consider what "Charb" said, paraphrasing a line sometimes attributed to Emiliano Zapata, hero of the Mexican Revolution: "I'd rather die on my feet than live on my knees."

. . .

Sherman Alexie is writing the best poetry of his life. That is my opinion, but I am not alone in holding it. Sherman's work was chosen for the last four editions of *The Best American Poetry*: by Kevin Young (2011), Mark Doty (2012), Denise Duhamel (2013) and Terrance Hayes (2014) in addition to his inclusion in *The Best of the Best* retrospective volume that Robert Pinsky edited in 2013. Alexie mixes colloquial diction and formal virtuosity; he uses forms—a narrative sequence of numbered sentences, a prose sonnet, a ghazal—to restrain and paradoxically to accentuate the power of raw emotion that his poems deliver.

Sherman's reputation goes far beyond the precincts of verse. He is celebrated for his fiction—*The Absolutely True Diary of a Part-Time Indian, The Lone Ranger and Tonto Fistfight in Heaven.* His prose has won him PEN prizes and a National Book Award. *Smoke Signals,* the movie he wrote, won accolades at the 1995 Sundance Festival. Just recently *Time* magazine rated *The Absolutely True Diary of a Part-Time Indian* as the "all-time" top young adult book, above *Harry Potter, Charlotte's Web, The Phantom Tollbooth,* and Judy Blume.[10]

But poetry has a special place in Alexie's prolific portfolio. It can be said of Sherman that poetry saved his life. An alcoholic trying to recover control, he went off the wagon on March 11, 1991. He binged; he behaved badly. But it was the last time he has had a drink. The next day he went to the mailbox and found a letter from Dick Lourie of Hanging Loose Press accepting a manuscript of Alexie's poems for publication. "There was a sign," Sherman says.

Sherman undertook the task of editing this volume with great zest, and he devoted himself tirelessly to scanning online journals, more of which are represented this year than ever before. In fact, more poems were chosen from the Academy of American Poets Poem-a-Day feature, skillfully edited by Alex Dimitrov, than from any other source. More magazines are represented altogether; fewer poems come from wide circulation journals or expected places. The spirit of democracy on display is nevertheless not inconsistent with the search for literary excellence.

There are those who expect our "hyphenated" poets to write obsessively or even exclusively about their identity and to demonstrate a degree of social responsibility to the group they represent. But Sherman's poetry rebuffs this patronizing expectation. A Spokane / Coeur d'Alene tribal member, Sherman grew up on a reservation and he has, as a result, a fertile source of subject matter. But his aim is to write good poems, not to represent a tribe, and he brings to his writing the exemplary qualities of intelligence and humor. Jessica Chapel of *The Atlantic* remarked that Alexie's characters wonder "what it means to be an Indian, what they are told it means to be an Indian, and how to present themselves as Indians both to whites and other Indians." Then the reporter asked the author: "Is this struggle or uncertainty endemic to the American Indian experience?"

"It's endemic to everybody's experience," Alexie replied. "I think we're all struggling with our identity. Literature is all about the search for identity, regardless of the ethnicity. Southern, New Yorker, black, white, Asian, immigrant—everyone's trying to find a sense of belonging. In *The Toughest Indian,* the journalist's primary struggle is not ethnic identity, but his sexuality. I don't think he knows any of his identities. One of the points I was trying to make in that story is that being Indian is just part of who we are. I suppose the big difference in Indian literature is that Indians are indigenous to this country, so all non-Indian literature could be seen as immigrant literature. The search for immigrant identity is much different than the search for indigenous identity, so I suppose if you're indigenous to a place and you're still searching for your identity, that's pretty ironic."[11]

Mark Strand, who died on November 29, 2014, was the guest editor of the 1991 volume in this series. At the time we worked together, he had completed *The Continuous Life* and was writing *Dark Harbor,* two of his best books. I was finishing *Signs of the Times,* my book on deconstruction and Paul de Man, cheered by Mark's support—

he loathed French critical theory and its effect on higher education. We would have long phone conversations twice a week or more to go over the poems that had come in and to talk about the shape of *The Best American Poetry 1991* as it evolved. We picked a Hopper for the cover; Mark was writing a book on him. As we went into production, he wrote a beautiful introductory essay that I had no trouble placing with *The New York Times Book Review*, which ran it on its front page. The series was still young enough that it seemed to demand all the attention we could give it, and we gave readings at Seton Hall University in New Jersey and at various New York locales. And then there were always bookstores to visit (the Strand!) or a Neil Welliver opening to attend as our friendship grew.

Mark was a connoisseur of poems—as of so many things, from wine and food to clothes and paintings. His work would give off a casual, even effortless feel, as if the poet (who had initially studied to be a painter) were possessed of a certain kind of natural grace, camouflaging all the craft and hard work. In *Dark Harbor*, he presents himself as a lucky man who knows the good life, striding on the pavement in his new dark blue double-breasted suit, lean and lanky, fresh after lunch at Lutece with his long-time editor. The picture is accurate. He was a poet of unusual glamour (light is "the mascara of Eden") and of romance. Yet, the prevailing feeling in the depth of his best work is melancholy. If mortality is our first and last problem, the need to say farewell is continuous. Death is the mother of beauty; poetry is a valediction forbidding mourning. A man and a woman—in one of Strand's late prose poems ("Provisional Eternity")—lie in bed. The man keeps saying "Just one more time." The woman wonders why he keeps saying that. "Because I never want it to end," he says. And what is it that he doesn't want to end? "This never wanting it to end." Farewell, friend.

CHAPTER THREE[12]

2016: "Surely some revelation is at hand . . ."

If our age is apocalyptic in mood—and rife with doomsday scenarios, nuclear nightmares, religious fanatics, and suicidal terrorists—there may be no more chilling statement of our condition than William Butler Yeats's poem, "The Second Coming." Written in 1919, in the immediate aftermath of the epoch-ending disaster that was World War I, "The Second Coming" extrapolates a fearful vision from the moral anarchy of the present. The poem also, almost incidentally, serves as an introduction to the great Irish poet's complex conception of history, which is cyclical, not linear. Things happen twice, the first time as sublime, the second time as horrifying, so that instead of the "second coming" of the savior Jesus Christ, Yeats envisages a monstrosity, a "rough beast" threatening violence commensurate with the human capacity for bloodletting.

Here is the poem:

Turning and turning in the widening gyre
The falcon cannot hear the falconer;
Things fall apart; the centre cannot hold;
Mere anarchy is loosed upon the world,
The blood-dimmed tide is loosed, and everywhere
The ceremony of innocence is drowned;
The best lack all conviction, while the worst
Are full of passionate intensity.

Surely some revelation is at hand;
Surely the Second Coming is at hand.
The Second Coming! Hardly are those words out
When a vast image out of *Spiritus Mundi*
Troubles my sight: somewhere in sands of the desert
A shape with lion body and the head of a man,
A gaze blank and pitiless as the sun,
Is moving its slow thighs, while all about it
Reel shadows of the indignant desert birds.
The darkness drops again; but now I know
That twenty centuries of stony sleep
Were vexed to nightmare by a rocking cradle,
And what rough beast, its hour come round at last,
Slouches towards Bethlehem to be born?

As a summary of the present age ("Things fall apart; the centre cannot hold; / Mere anarchy is loosed upon the world"), stanza one lays the groundwork for the vision spelled out in stanza two, which is as terrifying in its imagery as in its open-ended conclusion, the rhetorical question that makes it plain that a rough beast is approaching but leaves the monstrous details for us to fill.

As an instance of Yeats's epigrammatic ability, it is difficult to surpass the last two lines in the opening stanza: "The best lack all conviction, while the worst / Are full of passionate intensity." The aphorism retains its authority as an observation and a warning. Think of the absence of backbone with which certain right-minded individuals may be said to have met the threats of one bloody ism or another since the 1930s. Or consider our self-doubt and shaken confidence today, our lack of unity, the stalemate between rival factions. (In at least one sense, our House is divided against itself.) On the opposite side, Jihadists and advocates of sharia are rightly known for their extreme zealotry. All totalitarian regimes are based on dogma, and all dogmas demand of their followers a "passionate intensity" capable of overwhelming all other considerations.

Yeats works by magic. He has a system of myths and masks—based loosely on dreams, philosophy, occult studies, Celtic legend, and his wife's automatic writing—that he uses as the springboard for some of his poems. In a minute I will say something about his special vocabulary: the "gyre" in line one and "*Spiritus Mundi*" twelve lines later. But as a poet, I would prefer to place the emphasis on Yeats's craftsmanship. Note how he manages the transition from present to future, from things as they are to a vision of revolution and destruction, by a species of incantation. Line two of the second stanza ("Surely the Second Coming is at hand") is syntactically identical with line one ("Surely some revelation is at hand"), as if one phrase were a variant of the other. It is the second time in the poem that Yeats has managed this rhetorical maneuver. The first occurs in the opening stanza when the "blood-dimmed tide" replaces the "mere anarchy" that is "loosed" upon the world. In both cases, the second line intensifies the first by substituting something specific for something abstract or general.

The phrase "the Second Coming"—when repeated with the addition of an exclamation point—is enough to unleash the poet's visual imagination just as, in "Ode to a Nightingale," the word "forlorn" concluding the poem's penultimate stanza returns at the start of the final stanza, governing the dramatic final transition in Keats's poem. In "The Second Coming" the bestial image that follows from the repeated words, "A shape with lion body and the head of a man," is all the more terrifying because of the poet's craft: the metrical music of "A gaze blank and pitiless as the sun"; the unexpected adjectives ("indignant desert birds," "slow thighs"); the haunting pun ("Reel shadows"); the oddly gripping verb ("Slouches"); the rhetorical question that closes the poem like a prophecy that doubles as an admonition.

In a note written for a limited edition of his book *Michael Robartes and the Dancer*, Yeats explained that "*Spiritus Mundi*" (Latin for "spirit of the world") was his term for a "general storehouse of images," belonging to everyone and no one. It functions a little like Jung's collective unconscious and is the source for the "vast image" in "The Second Coming." Yeats writes in his introduction to his play "The Resurrection" that he often saw such an image, "always at my left side just out of the range of sight, a brazen winged beast that I associated with laughing, ecstatic destruction."

As for "gyre" (pronounced with a hard "g"), in Yeats's system it is a sort of ideogram for history. In essays on Yeats, I have seen the gyres—two of them always—pictured sometimes vertically, in the shape of an hourglass, and sometimes horizontally, as a pair of interpenetrating triangles that resemble inverted stars of David. The gyre represents a cycle lasting 2,000 years.

But I maintain that knowledge of the poet's esoterica (as set forth in his book *A Vision*) is, though fascinating, unnecessary. Nor does the reader need to know much about falconry, a medieval sport beloved of the European nobility, to understand that there has been a breakdown in communications when the "falcon cannot hear the falconer."

Read "The Second Coming" aloud and you will see its power as oratory. And ask yourself which unsettles you more: the revolutionary monster "slouching toward Bethlehem" or the sad truth that the best of us don't want to get involved, while the worst know no restraint in their pursuit of power?

I have begun my foreword with Yeats's poem for two reasons. The first is that I can think of few works so eerily prophetic—and so apt for us today. The second is that we who work on *The Best American Poetry* mean to honor the great poems of the past even as we celebrate the vitality of verse in our time.

. . .

Edward Hirsch was my choice to edit the anthology this year because my admiration of his poems is matched by my respect for his skills as a critic, a teacher, and a judge—all that goes into the editing of an annual anthology that does its best to promote the art itself and showcase some of the poems that have moved or amused us. When Kobe Bryant announced his retirement from basketball with a poem, I thought of "Fast Break," one of the highlights of Hirsch's *Wild Gratitude*, which won the National Book Critics Circle prize in 1987. "Fast Break" consists of one sentence stretched across thirty-six lines beginning with a hook shot that "kisses the rim and / hangs there helplessly, but doesn't drop" to the other side of the court where the power forward makes his layup but falls to the floor "with a wild, headlong motion / for the game he loved like a country // and swiveling back to see an orange blur / floating perfectly through the net."

In his career as a professor (at the University of Houston) and an administrator (President of the Guggenheim Foundation), Eddie has found a way to blend the tasks of pedagogy and critical judgment while relentlessly pursuing his passion for poetry. He has won widespread acclaim most recently for his book about the death of his son, *Gabriel: A Poem* (Knopf, 2014). At the same time, he has written about poetry in essays and reviews, columns filed on a weekly deadline (*The Washington Post*), and an ambitious *Poet's Glossary* (Houghton Mifflin Harcourt, 2014); he has found time to edit a slender volume devoted to the nightingale in poetry, to introduce an anthology emanating from the Academy of American Poets' Poem-a-Day project, and to keep a demanding travel schedule. We compared notes and enthusiasms frequently, and I know it gave him great pleasure that a significant number of poets in this volume have never previously appeared in *The Best American Poetry*.

Important poets have died since the 2015 edition of this anthology. Philip Levine, C. K. Williams, Claudia Emerson, and James Tate are four whose work appears in this year's *BAP*. I feel a special sorrow at the passing of Jim Tate, who was guest editor of the 1997 volume. I got to talk to Jim on the phone regularly during the whole of 1996 and felt like a partner in the making of a brilliant anthology. He was real—he spoke mildly but knew what he wanted poetry to do. In his own work he was funny, very funny—funny, seemingly without effort. He helped people realize that humor is as compatible with the lyric impulse as the metaphysical wit of seventeenth-century poets such as Donne and Marvell. And he continually widened the possibilities of poetry in prose.

My favorite memory of Jim is from early May 2001. Jim and Dara Wier had organized and were hosting the Juniper Festival at the University of Massachusetts in Amherst. They invited me to be the keynote speaker. One evening, Dara hosted a party at her place and invited my wife Stacey and me to come. I asked Jim for directions. "Would you like me to draw a map for you?" he asked.

"That would be good," I said.

"Look at my palm," he said, turning up his right hand and using a left-hand finger as a pointer.

I looked at his palm and suddenly we were in a James Tate poem.

"Do you see this line?" he said.

"Yes," I said. "It's your lifeline."

"Well," he said, "you go up this line and then you hang a left up here."

"How long will it take?" I asked.

"Not long," he said.

And the amazing thing is . . . on the basis of these directions . . . we got there. Safe and sound.

CHAPTER FOUR[13]

2017: "Outside the Gates of Eden."

If in January 2016, someone had told you that in the year ahead the Cubs will win the World Series, Bob Dylan will win the Nobel Prize for literature, and Donald Trump will be elected president of the United States, you'd have thought that person batty. Yet all these things have come to pass, and at least one of them has a direct bearing on poetry.

No sooner was it announced that Dylan has become the first American Nobel laureate in literature since Toni Morrison than the quarrels began. Enthusiasts cited the way Dylan has entered and modified the culture. How his phrases linger in the air: The times they are a-changin'. There are no truths outside the Gates of Eden. You don't need a weatherman to know which way the wind blows. He not busy being born is busy dying.

But the cries of dismay were predictable if only because the poetry community is divided, and because there is an unhealthy amount of bile and resentment out there. Any American poet—even our grand old master Richard Wilbur, now 96—would get his share of Bronx cheers if he were to win the Nobel. It was said of Dylan that he didn't need the prize, that he is yet another old white guy, that he is arrogant, that he composes songs not poems, or is "at best," as one disgruntled observer put it, "a pretentious high-school-notebook poet"—in other words, not a poet at all.

Purists would say that what Dylan writes are lyrics, which

depend on their musical setting for coherence and are inextricably bound up with their performance. I would counter that the best of Dylan's songs work on the page, not only because of their originality, but equally because they constitute the autobiography of a fascinating, shape-shifting personality that is rebellious, ornery, intense, and has proved remarkably attuned to the zeitgeist.

With the most prescient timing in recent publishing history, *Bob Dylan: The Lyrics 1961-2012* appeared within one month of the prize announcement in October. The book contains the words of all of Dylan's songs, organized album by album from his eponymous 1962 debut to his most recent efforts. The transcendent period was the stretch between 1964 and 1967—the period of "Like a Rolling Stone," "Desolation Row," "Sad-Eyed Lady of the Lowlands," "Visions of Johanna," "Just Like a Woman" and "All Along the Watchtower.' While the lyrics and their reception make the primary case for Dylan's achievement, I believe that *Chronicles* (2004), the first volume of his projected three-volume memoirs, offers a valuable window into the writer's brain. "Truth was the last thing on my mind, and even if there was such a thing, I didn't want it in my house," he wrote of trying to compose songs. "Oedipus went looking for the truth and when he found it, it ruined him. It was a cruel horror of a joke. So much for the truth. I was gonna talk out of both sides of my mouth and what you heard depended on which side you were standing. If I ever did stumble on any truth, I was gonna sit on it and keep it down."

A self-creation in the tradition of Jay Gatsby rather than that of Julius Henry Marx (i.e., Groucho), Bob discarded his birth name (Zimmerman) in favor of the moniker of the wild, word-drunk Welsh poet Dylan Thomas. A natural surrealist with bardic leanings, Dylan radiated a kind of Bohemian glamour. The lyrics reflect the stance of a put-on artist, a joker, enigmatic, elusive and full of insolence or righteous belligerence. "Maggie's Farm" (1965) elevates "I quit" into poetry: He "hands you a nickel, / He hands you a dime, /

He asks you with a grin / If you're havin' a good time, / Then he fines you every time you slam the door / I ain't gonna work for Maggie's brother no more." Or consider the ire hurled at the false friend in "Positively 4th Street": "I wish that for just one time / You could stand inside my shoes / You'd know what a drag it is / To see you."

Usually when I discuss Bob Dylan as a poet, I point to his visionary songs. "Desolation Row" (1965), which I selected for inclusion in *The Oxford Book of American Poetry,* is terrific in its phantasmagoria. The title song of *Highway 61 Revisited* (1965) begins with God and Abraham mixing it up in Genesis 22: "God said to Abraham, 'Kill me a son' / Abe says, 'Man, you must be puttin' me on.'" The allusions here and elsewhere in Dylan's lyrics—in which at any moment Genghis Kahn or F. Scott Fitzgerald might put in an appearance—look random but are pointed and shrewd. Still, the case for Dylan rests as much on his powers of rhetoric as on his oracular powers. Some of his strongest lines are infused with the spirit of protest: "How many years can a mountain exist, / Before it's washed to the sea?" Others verge on heartbreak ("It don't even matter to me where you're wakin' up tomorrow / But, mama, you're just on my mind") or celebrate a lazy day in an easy chair ("Buy me a flute / And a gun that shoots / Tailgates and substitutes / Strap yourself to the tree with roots / You ain't goin' nowhere"). He can bring a dream to a close with the inevitability of a rhyme: "the pumps don't work / 'cause the vandals took the handles." The rhymes in "Like a Rolling Stone" and "I Want You" show there's a lot of life left in that venerable device.

In 1880, Matthew Arnold brought to the study of poetry the concept of "touchstones" for exemplary lines that imprint themselves on the mind. It is a criterion the author of "Visions of Johanna" (1966) meets. "The ghost of 'lectricity howls in the bones of her face." With or without music, that line sings. Only a true poet could have written it.

A larger issue emerged in the Dylan debates: what qualifies as "literature"? Dylan's own response was to retreat into modesty. He didn't go to Sweden to collect the prize but sent a banquet speech. It was hard to process the news, he wrote, but then he "began to think about William Shakespeare, the great literary figure. I would reckon he thought of himself as a dramatist. The thought that he was writing literature couldn't have entered his head. His words were written for the stage—meant to be spoken not read. When he was writing *Hamlet*, I'm sure he was thinking about a lot of different things: 'Who're the right actors for these roles?' 'How should this be staged?' 'Do I really want to set this in Denmark?' His creative vision and ambitions were no doubt at the forefront of his mind, but there were also more mundane matters to consider and deal with. 'Is the financing in place?' Are there enough good seats for my patrons?' 'Where am I going to get a human skull?' I would bet that the farthest thing from Shakespeare's mind was the question 'Is this *literature*?'" These are all fair points, I reckon, though it should be noted that in making them, Dylan manages to compare himself to "William Shakespeare, the great literary figure."

The choice of Dylan for the Nobel has set a precedent for widening the category of "literature" to embrace the work of other troubadours (and in future, perhaps, filmmakers and showrunners). *The New Yorker* has showcased the poetry of Leonard Cohen, who died at eighty-two just weeks after an impressive profile by David Remnick appeared in the magazine. I am happy that Natasha Trethewey chose a Leonard Cohen poem for this year's *Best American Poetry*. "California Poem," a poem by Johnny Cash that *The New Yorker* published in September, didn't make the cut, but it did reinforce the notion that the boundary between poems and lyrics is not an impossible one to cross. And when Lin-Manuel Miranda accepted the Tony Award for his colossally successful musical play *Hamilton* with a "16-line sonnet," it came as a reminder that verse continues to lend prestige to a formal occasion, be it a wedding or an award ceremony. And yet—

. . .

Ours is a great era for hate—what George Orwell called "a human barrel-organ shooting propaganda at you by the hour. The same thing over and over again. Hate, hate, hate. Let's get all together and have a good hate." These sentences are from his novel *Coming up for Air* (1939) in the course of which our protagonist, a middle-aged man with an expanding waistline, gets frustrated trying to explain to a philosopher friend, an aesthete, why it's important to fight Hitler.

Now and then there's an odd news story demonstrating that the subject of poetry can lead to a display of high passion, even a fistfight or a duel. In September 2016, *The Independent* reported that in the town of Irbit in the Ural Mountains in Russia, a vodka-soaked advocate of poetry killed a prose partisan in a brawl over the rival merits of the literary genres each championed. (A month earlier, in an argument over the philosophy of Immanuel Kant, one man shot another in a grocery store in southern Russia.) Reduce the amount of alcohol and raise the amount of bitterness, and you arrive at the state of critical discourse at its worst. In *The Big Short*, an entertaining and instructive movie about the financial shenanigans that led to the near collapse of Wall Street in 2008, these lines appear on the screen: "Overheard in a Washington, D.C. Bar: Truth is poetry, and people fucking hate poetry." That is a far cry from Keats's "Beauty is truth, truth beauty," but beauty is out of favor, and paranoia and hatred have risen in its stead. Joel Stein, *Time* magazine's humorist, wrote a cover story on "the culture of hate" and how it is taking over the Internet. The Internet multiplies the avenues, conceals the perpetrators, loosens the restraints. There are a lot of mischief makers and propagandists out there, and the 24/7 need for news stories on cable TV keeps the hysteria level high. Keats wrote that "the Imagination is a monastery and I am its monk." Wallace Stevens exalted the imagination as superior to unredeemable actuality.

That is a lot of to expect of the poetic imagination. But the possibility helps to shelter you from the corrosiveness of public discourse.

Of all the arts, poetry may attract the most venomous haters and the most persistent predictors of its decay and inevitable demise. Ben Lerner argues, in *The Hatred of Poetry* (2016), that hatred itself is part and parcel of the creative impulse. "Poetry and the hatred of poetry are for me—and maybe for you—inextricable," he says. On the surface, this may seem perverse, an internalizing of the dismissive things people say (or don't say but think) about poetry. But it is possible, as Lerner suggests, that the famous opening line of Marianne Moore's "Poetry"—"I, too, dislike it"—is every poet's starting point or governing condition. Poets are control freaks with a strong streak of perfectionism and by their own standards can never be satisfied with their work. The best poem is the one that has not yet been written.

As a Platonic idealist, Lerner has insightful things to say: "Socrates is the wisest of all people because he knows he knows nothing; Plato is a poet who stays closest to poetry because he refuses actual poems." Lerner argues that defenses of poetry going back to Sir Philip Sidney tend to assert "an ideal of imaginative literature" rather than to exalt individual poems. The discrepancy between the ideal and the actual poem widens. The poet as idealist finds all poetry defective. The killer, as Lerner sees it, is the demand for universality, for "the intensely subjective, personal poem" that can somehow "authentically encompass everyone." Such a poem "is an impossibility in a world characterized by difference and violence."

The question, however, is whether such idealism is common to all poets, and is it the primary standard that poets adopt while working on poems? Are poets, then, doomed to the melancholy of certain failure? The failure of poets "to be universal, to speak to and for everyone in the manner of Whitman" is neither a realistic goal nor necessarily a wise one. On the contrary, as Lerner notes, it is the logic behind foolish articles alleging the decline of poetry. It might also be said that there is a difference between Lerner's title and Marianne Moore's statement. The "too" in "I, too, dislike it" slyly suggests a likeness, a secret alliance between writer and reader. We mistrust poetry, we know it is full of false sentiments and insincere rhetoric, and so we have to be won over. Less aggressive than "hate," "dislike" may be the more accurate term. It may come closer to the "perfect contempt" that poets instinctively display when addressing specimens of the art not their own. Using words from the same poem by Marianne Moore, we might argue further that poetry is in service not to an emotion or state of mind, but to the quest for a certain kind of power, the power to create "imaginary gardens with real gardens in hem."

Not a writer of poetry himself, George Orwell was impatient with poetry for quite different reasons. Of what use could it be against a machine gun? "Ours is a civilization in which the very word 'poetry' evokes a hostile snigger or, at best, the sort of frozen disgust that most people feel when they hear the word 'God,'" Orwell wrote in 1942. "Poetry is disliked because it is associated with unintelligibility, intellectual pretentiousness and a general feeling of Sunday-on-a-weekday," he wrote a year later.[14]

Do "people fucking hate poetry," as *The Big Short* announces? Do they put up with poets as the slightly comic figures on the college faculty who do their part for the good of the community by teaching poetry in old age homes and penitentiaries? My own view of things is that a poet can expect not hate but 'unremitting indifference / broken up by patches of hostility."[15] "Barely tolerated, living on the margin / In our technological society": the opening of John Ashbery's poem "Soonest Mended" (1970) characterizes the poet's condition.[16]

And yet it sometimes seems as if everyone has a niece or nephew who writes poetry. Ben Lerner has an amusing passage about what happens when a poet is unwise enough to reveal his or her vocation to a total stranger on an airplane. Lerner writes that the embarrassment is double: "There is embarrassment for the poet—couldn't you get a real job and put your childish ways behind you?—but there is also embarrassment on the part of the non-poet because having to acknowledge one's total alienation from poetry chafes against the early association of poetry and self."

W. H. Auden's solution to the problem of identifying himself to temporary companions was to say that he was a medieval historian. "It withers curiosity," he explained.[17]

. . .

In *The Best American Poetry 2017*, we have three Youngs (C. Dale, Dean, and Kevin) and an Olds. We have sonnets, several of them in rhyme; a list poem; a poem in rhymed haiku stanzas; a poem in the manner of a text message; an epithalamium, and a verse epistle "To Marlon Brando in Hell." We have a master in his eighties, and a Stuyvesant High School alumna who was born in 1997, when this anthology series was in its tenth year. Most unusually, we have a poem, R. T. Smith's "Maricon," that treats the March 1962 fight between boxers Emily Griffith and Benny ("the Kid") Paret—the same bout that triggered Donald Platt's poem "The Main Event," which appeared in *The Best American Poetry 2015*.

Natasha Trethewey, the guest editor of this volume, appeared for the first time in *The Best American Poetry* in 2000. That year her first book, *Domestic Work*, assembled evidence of an ability to find the dualities of her personal history mirrored ironically but pointedly in the language that we speak. As the daughter of a white man and an African-American woman in Mississippi at a time when interracial marriages were against the law, she could identify herself with the "mixed girl" in the 1959 movie *Imitation of Life*. She grew up, she writes, "light-bright, near-white, / high-yellow, red-boned, / in a black place"—and was gifted at telling "white lies." In 2007, Trethewey won the Pulitzer Prize for *Native Guard*, her third book. To the poet's repertoire, the book added the challenges of poetic form. The title poem—the journal of a black soldier from a Louisiana regiment of freed slaves in the Civil War—consists of ten unrhymed sonnets. The last line of each is mirrored and distorted in the first line of the next. The effect is complex: smooth continuity, elegant circularity, but also a third thing that disturbs the peace and order of the other two. The poem begins, "Truth be told, I do not want to forget." It ends with "a scaffolding of bone / we tread upon, forgetting. Truth be told." The poem exists precisely in the space between those two poles.

In 2012, Natasha was named Poet Laureate of the United States. She has held faculty appointments at Duke, Chapel Hill, Yale, Emory, and now Northwestern. Her list of favorite poems from 2016 grew slowly. "Mostly I want to be blown away when I read a poem," she told me. The poems she chose had to meet that strict criterion. Not the reputation of the poet but the poem on the page was what mattered. Numerous magazines were consulted. On the honor roll, *The Kenyon Review* and *Ploughshares* are tied on top of the list: more poems were chosen from them, five each, than from any other single source. The subjects addressed in the poems include Aleppo, God, the life you didn't lead, "Girl from the North Country" as sung by Bob Dylan and Johnny Cash, grackles, the seventeenth century, a wristwatch, the "age of anxiety," deconstruction, and "the post-galactic abyss of sex with strangers" (Major Jackson), to limit myself to ten. The table of contents includes the work of poets who are entirely new to me as well as poets we have showcased before.

Sometimes a poem goes viral, usually to the surprise of the author. One poem that went viral in 2016 you'll find in the pages of this year's anthology: Maggie Smith's "Good Bones." It is probably safe to say that no poem last year had quite the effect of a piece of doggerel that a political satirist recited on a TV show in Germany about the controversial president of Turkey. The poem touched on President Recep Tayyip Erdogan's anatomy, his alleged interest in barnyard animals, and the athletically demanding sexual activities he supposedly enjoys doing with them. The effort was in the category of the crude and puerile. Nevertheless, the Turkish president was not amused; the poem caused a minor diplomatic flap between Germany and Turkey, and quite a lot of snarky comment. The incident made me think of a piece of light verse that doubled as a political poem of some brilliance and bite. The writer was the late Robert Conquest, historian of Soviet Russia, author of *The Great Terror: Stalin's Purge of the Thirties*. The poem stretches the form of the limerick, disdaining crudities. In five lines, Conquest sums up several decades of revolutionary Russian history: 'There was a great Marxist called Lenin, / Who did two or three million men in. / That's a lot to have done in, / But where he did one in / That grand Marxist Stalin did ten in."[18]

CHAPTER FIVE[19]

2018: "Poetry is philosophy's sister, the one that wears makeup."

In 2017, one former guest editor of *The Best American Poetry* succeeded another when Kevin Young (BAP 2011) was hired to take the place of Paul Muldoon (BAP 2005) as poetry editor of *The New Yorker*. Paul, who continues to teach at Princeton, is the co-author, with Jean Hanff Korelitz, of a critically acclaimed recreation of the holiday feast in James Joyce's "The Dead." And for the first time in a decade, he is eligible to grace *The New Yorker* with a poetic tour de force on the order of "Aubade," which ran in the January 29, 2018 issue.

As for Kevin, he left his post at Emory University to head the Schomburg Center for Research in Black Culture in New York City, where his first public appearances celebrated the Schomburg's acquisition of James Baldwin's archives ("a well-timed coup," said *The New York Times*) and the life and legacy of tenor saxophonist Sonny Rollins, who used to practice on New York's Williamsburg Bridge (because no one complained about the noise), and for whom the bridge may someday be named.

For an admiring profile of Kevin Young that ran in *Esquire*, Robert Baird asked David Remnick, the editor of *The New Yorker*, who hired Young, why *The New Yorker* "still publishes poems," as if that were a quixotic or archaic thing to do. "Poetry is arguably, in some compressed and magical fashion, the highest form of expression, the greatest devotion we have to our most intricate invention, language itself," Remnick wrote in an email. "How can we publish a magazine that proposes to be literary, as well as journalistic, that does not publish poetry?"[20]

The title *Esquire's* editors affixed to Baird's piece—"Can Kevin Young Make Poetry Matter Again?"—echoes that of the essay Dana Gioia wrote for *The Atlantic* in 1991: "Can Poetry Matter?" In reaction to this echo, one can 1) revert to adage (*plus ça change, plus c'est la meme chose*), or 2) exclaim over the persistence of the worry, which seems to have outlived the related anxiety that either the novel or the author is dead, or 3) linger over some paradoxes. Perhaps never before have so many people written poetry despite the universally acknowledged truth that few folks buy poetry books. "It is almost eerie, the number of people who want to be poets," Louise Glück remarked when working on *The Best American Poetry 1993*, and the number has gone up in the twenty-five years since. An academic industry has grown around the teaching of poetry and other forms of creative writing, yet voices keep proclaiming that poetry is ready for the morgue, has forfeited its public responsibility, has lost its audience, has slid into irrelevance. A survey released by the National Endowment for the Arts in 2015 provides statistics to back up the gloom-and-doomsayers out there. If your idea of an active public is anyone who has read "at least one poem" in a calendar year, that public declined precipitously in the ten-year period ending in 2012 and is limited to 6.7 per cent of the population. Do the math and you still get a hefty number of people—until you remind yourself of how broad the category is and how low the figure would be if people were asked to name a living poet or to recite a couple of lines of verse.

Robert Baird, author of the *Esquire* piece, has written one of the most cogent critiques of, or laments for poetry today. (There are plenty of bad ones.) "Spend It All" appeared on the *Best American Poetry* blog on January 12, 2012. The post begins with an arresting observation: "Pass much time in the company of poets—young or old, online or off—and soon enough you'll find yourself privy to the cycles of consternation and dismay inspired by the general insignificance of poetry." This is undeniable even if one reflexively counters with the observation that America can now boast of having more poets per capita than ever in its history. Poetry has "slipped beyond decadence" into an eccentricity. "Poetry lost the common reader a long time ago, if it ever had her, and from where I sit, it seems well on its way to losing the uncommon reader as well," Baird writes. "Time was you had to know at least a little Larkin or Lowell or Creeley to count yourself a cultured intellectual, just as older times demanded you had to keep current with opera and ballet. No more. These days we feel like we're shouldering our share of the civilizational burden if we keep up our subscription to *The New York Times* and pledge yearly to NPR." It sounds despairing, but Baird keeps his cool. "If you're a poet you decide that there are too many poems that need writing, far too many that need reading. Plus, you figure, if people don't like poetry, then bully for them, just like Frank O'Hara said all those years ago. Poetry, like virtue, is its own reward." Then, too, he concludes, with the fortitude of Tennyson's Ulysses, there is such a thing as "literary magnificence."[21]

Everyone has always wanted to be a poet. The desire to write poetry, to live the life of a poet, has a long and honorable tradition. Here, from "The Fall of Hyperion," is Keats's statement of the theme:

Who alive can say,
"Thou art no Poet may'st not tell thy dreams?"
Since every man whose soul is not a clod
Hath visions, and would speak, if he had loved
And been well nurtured in his mother tongue.

Whether the dream now purpos'd to rehearse
Be poet's or fanatic's will be known
When this warm scribe my hand is in the grave.

Keats anticipated Freud, who established the rationale for the argument that there is a poet in each of us. If the unconscious is the true genius, if it is the source of the dreams, the errors, and the jokes that prefigure poems, then all who dream, who err, who jest can get into the action in this game that has few and mostly lenient referees, and what's the harm? If there is even a slim chance that the amateur poet, the student poet, the Sunday poet may participate in the cultural heritage that nourishes the imagination and resists the mighty forces of materialism, isn't that all the justification we need to encourage the multitudes to write poetry and prose?

There is a flip side. Lack of talent or inspiration hasn't stopped a lot of Shagpats from getting in on the action.[22] A good heart and the power of positive thinking can take the poetaster a long way. Social media accelerate the tendency. The queen of Instagram poets is Rupi Kaur, a Canadian woman born in India. She has two books and 1.5 million followers on Instagram. She also has cash customers. Two and a half million copies of *Milk and Honey*, her first book, have been sold. Her poems, signed with her name in lower case, are sincere, well-meaning, and sensitive in the approved way of greeting card verse. According to *New York* magazine, Queen Rupi reigns in "the realm of college freshwomen who have recently been or may soon go through breakups." Carl Wilson of *The New York Times* defines her target audience as consisting of readers "who may think of poetry as the literary equivalent of opera or ballet, a privileged white-male establishment hostile to their interests." Covering the "inevitable backlash against Instagram's favourite poet" for the *Guardian*, Priya Khaira-Hanks writes that Kaur and some of her rivals "hit upon a winning formula: rupturing short confessional pieces with erratic line breaks to share hard-won truths." Example: "if you are not enough for yourself / you will never be enough / for someone else." In *The Wall Street Journal,* the headline of Nina Sovich's piece on the Rupi Kaur phenomenon—which lacked a single line of Kaur's poetry—summed it up. "My Love Is Like a Hashtag: 'Instagram Poets' Sell well."[23] The last best defense of such verse is that it may serve as a "gateway" to the real stuff. I can give lip service to this proposition even as I note that it sometimes seems as if the only time articles about poetry appear prominently in the culture pages of our newspapers is when the subject is a counterfeit, the implication being that we'd be prepared to embrace poetry if only it weren't poetry.

Just as it occurs to me that the self-erase function of Snapchat may make it an exemplary medium, Mark Bibbins lets me know that William Carlos Williams's "This Is Just To Say" has become "a meme on Twitter, with people posting parodies/variations—some of which are receiving thousands of likes/retweets." In Williams's sly poem, the speaker confesses to eating the plums in the icebox that "you" were planning to have for breakfast. "Forgive me" he says, but what follows sounds more like a gloat than an apology. The plums, he explains, "were delicious, so sweet and so cold." Kenneth Koch, a master parodist, took Williams's formula to a logical extreme in four "variations." The last of the four epitomizes the comic sublime, packing an exclamatory surprise in each line: "Last night we went dancing and I broke your leg. / Forgive me. I was clumsy, / And I wanted you here in the wards, where I am the doctor!"

I have used the fake apology as a prompt in my classes at the New School and in the weekly *Next Line, Please* challenges on the website of *The American Scholar,* so it didn't altogether surprise me to learn that the fake apology was causing a Twitter ruckus. Many of the entries, seemingly composed off the cuff, turned the case of the eaten plums into new lyrics for familiar poems or jingles in the public domain. A writer self-characterized as "Medusa without frontiers" and "Ophelia in waders" opted for an Emily Dickinson locution: "Because I would not stop for plums, / I ate all yours, you see. / And now the icebox holds just pits; / I'm sorry. –Willie C." Sir Ian modeled his entry on the opening of Allen Ginsberg's "Howl": "I saw the best plums of my generation destroyed by Williams, starving hysterical naked, / dragging himself through the icebox shelves at dawn looking for a sweet cold fix."[24]

You may say: If this is poetry, what happened to language charged with meaning? Where are the best words in the best order? Is this what Wallace Stevens had in mind when he wrote that poetry is "a means of redemption," "a search for the inexplicable," "the renovation of experience," and, just to keep you on your toes, "a pheasant disappearing in the bush"? Does this do what Emily Dickinson prescribed—take your head off? The prosecution rests.

In chambers, the judge reminds counsel that the gallant thing is to change the subject and end the paragraph on a positive note. And the jury is addressed as one poet talking to another, trying to define the indefinable. Though judgment is subjective, and rankings are best left to posterity, the inevitably unsuccessful attempt to define poetry can help us to grasp its essence and recognize the genuine article when it comes along. "Poetry is language that sounds better and means more," in Charles Wright's formulation. "Poetry is philosophy's sister, the one that wears makeup," says Jennifer Grotz. Paradoxes please us: "a poem is an interruption of silence, whereas prose is a continuation of noise" (Billy Collins). Poetry is a game—and it is also a lover's quarrel with the world of words. Then it occurs to me: substitute "America" or "paradise" for "poetry" in that formulation, and the game gets even more interesting. America is a melting pot, or it's the land of the free agent. Paradise is always being lost or maybe it's a version of the place where, when you have to go there, they have to take you in. Poetry is a cafe, or it's the place where parallel lines cross, or up close it's the gibbous mirrored eye of an insect.

. . .

Dana Gioia and I have been friends since we met in 1982. I know of no one more dedicated to literature and the arts in the largest sense: he loves to read and talk about poetry, and he is equally passionate and knowing about theater, opera, jazz, and painting. After a fling at Harvard as a graduate student in literature, Dana went to business school at Stanford and joined the ranks of maverick poets who earned their living in business or a profession rather than in academe. By day he worked for General Foods, but he managed to publish poems and ambitious essays in magazines such as *The Hudson Review*. He became a leader of the New Formalism, a movement determined to restore to poetry the importance formerly placed on rhyme, meter, and traditional form. He also translated Montale, helped make the case for the underrated Weldon Kees, and wrote touching personal memoirs about Elizabeth Bishop (whom he had come to know while at Harvard) and John Cheever.

After giving up his business career to give more time to the literary life, Dana wrote poems and essays and opera libretti, edited textbooks and anthologies, translated Seneca, collaborated with all sorts of folks on all sorts of worthy projects. But he had another surprise in store for us. In 2003, he became the chairman of the National Endowment for the Arts, in which capacity he served for six years. When he took the helm, the organization was in bad odor. In a burst of energy, he refashioned its image and resuscitated its reputation. He launched initiatives to enlarge the readership for serious literature ("The Big Read"); to promote the memorization of verse ("Poetry Out Loud"); to provide "creative art therapy" to returning veterans ("Operation Homecoming"); to produce Shakespeare plays in untraditional venues, such as military bases; and to contrive new ways to celebrate our heroes of opera and jazz. And he managed to sell the arts to congressmen not necessarily disposed to be supportive.

It is safe to say that not since Archibald MacLeish headed the Library of Congress has a poet worked so hard, and accomplished so much of value, in so prominent a position in the federal government. Not everyone can see beyond his or her essential understanding of poetry to be able to acknowledge the legitimacy of rival conceptions. Dana has that ability, and in this book, has done his best to represent the remarkable variety to be found in American poetry at its best in 2018.

. . .

We lost two titans in 2017: at the age of ninety, John Ashbery died on September 3; Richard Wilbur passed on October 14, aged ninety-six.

A graduate of Amherst College (class of 1942), Dick Wilbur served during World War II with the 36th Infantry Division. He saw action in Italy, France, and Germany. Upon his return, he taught at his alma mater and at Harvard, Wellesley, Wesleyan, and Smith. He liked living in the country. With his wife, Charlee, to whom he was devoted, he lived in Cummington, Massachusetts, birthplace of William Cullen Bryant, and spent many springs in Key West, Florida. In 2004, his *Collected Poems 1943-2004* appeared from Harcourt. Twice he won the Pulitzer Prize. He wrote lyrics for Leonard Bernstein's *Candide*, and his translations from seventeenth century French drama (Molière, Racine, Corneille) are performed widely. Wilbur's mastery of rhetoric and command of poetic form is or should be self-evident to all who have wrestled with words and their meanings. In his poems he weds deep humane intelligence with superb technique and unfailing fealty to the ideals of beauty and truth. "A poem should not be like a Double-Crostic; it should not be the sort of puzzle in which you get nothing until you get it all," he wrote. "Art does not or should not work that way; we are not cheated of a symphony if we fail to react to some passage on the flute, and a good poem should yield itself more than once, offering the reader an early and sure purchase, and deepening repeatedly as he comes to know it better."

Dick was the most genial and gracious of individuals. I profited from his expertise on many subjects: Edgar Allan Poe, the great American songbook, French classical tragedy, May Swenson, riddles, the haiku stanza put to narrative or expository use. Twelve guest editors in this series have selected Wilbur's poems. His contributor's note in *The Best American Poetry 1999* concluded: "His several books for children have amused some adults." There then followed this comment on his poem "This Pleasing, Anxious Being": "I think that people resist as long as they can a full sense of the world's change and of their own aging. At last, when a certain number of irreplaceable people are gone, and the home place has been razed, and one is the only rememberer of certain things, the gut acknowledges what the mind has always thought it knew. That is the source of this poem, which moves both back and forward in time, and considers time in several perspectives. The title is taken from the twenty-second stanza of Gray's 'Elegy.'"

Three days before John Ashbery died, my wife and I saw *Marjorie Prime,* Michael Almereyda's fine movie, with an all-star cast (Jon Hamm, Geena Davis, Lois Smith) and wonderful samplings of a Beethoven string quartet, Poulenc, Mozart, "I Shall Be Released," and the dialogue of *Casablanca*. But the highlight of *Marjorie Prime* occurs when the character played by Tim Robbins reads aloud a love letter addressed to his mother-in-law, now deceased, said to have been written by a tennis-playing French-Canadian suitor who expresses the usual sentiments then abruptly switches to the first six lines of John Ashbery's "At North Farm":

> Somewhere someone is traveling furiously toward you,
> At incredible speed, traveling day and night,
> Through blizzards and desert heat,
> across torrents, through narrow passes.
> But will he know where to find you,
> Recognize you when he sees you,
> Give you the thing he has for you?

I phoned John the next evening to tell him of our pleasure in hearing these lines. Aside from an intermittent cough, John sounded like John, and it gives me pleasure to report that he remained his witty, droll, clever, charming self right up to the end. A few days later I was writing copy in the past tense.

John was a mentor to me and a good friend. I went to readings he gave in my sophomore year at Columbia and was, like many of my classmates, blown away by his long poem "The Skaters," which many of my buddies on the *Columbia Review*, committed as we were to the aesthetic of the New York School, thought was the single finest long poem in English since "The Waste Land." He very quickly became my favorite poet.

Some of his friends called him Ashes. I favored JA in part because of his brilliant early poem "The Picture of Little JA in a Prospect of Flowers," the title of which was itself a lift from a poem by Andrew Marvell. We—those of us privileged enough to get close to the man—would entertain one another with anecdotes about him, clever things he said, or just news of a great new poem, such as "Self-Portrait in a Convex Mirror," which knocked our socks off when it appeared in *Poetry* magazine in 1974. A year later, it was the title poem of a poetry collection that went on to capture the Pulitzer Prize, the National Book Award, and the National Book Critics Circle Award, an unprecedented triple crown.

It was my great good luck that our professional paths crossed three significant times in the 1970s and '80s. John and I shared an office at Brooklyn College the year I taught there. Later, when I reviewed books for *Newsweek*, John was the magazine's art critic. And when I launched *The Best American Poetry* series in 1988 with Scribner, JA was our first guest editor. So, it was not only as a poet, but also as a teacher, a critic, a journalist, and an editor that he inspired me.

My lifelong devotion to John's work is reflected in the book I edited in 1980, *Beyond Amazement: New Essays on John Ashbery*, and in my book about the formative years of the New York School, *The Last Avant-Garde* (1998). In 1984 Harvey Shapiro of *The New*

York Times Magazine phoned and commissioned a profile for the magazine's "creative mind" series. I'm glad I got to interview John formally, though I never met anyone cagier. To simulate a conversation with him in public, which we did several times, required ingenuity and the willingness to look foolish. Sometimes things he said in interviews entered the general discourse. "Often people don't listen to you when you speak to them. It's only when you talk to yourself that they prick up their ears." And: "I am aware of the pejorative associations of the word 'escapist,' but I insist that we need all the escapism we can get and even that isn't going to be enough."

Strikingly different in many particulars, Ashbery and Wilbur have in common a profound understanding of English and American poetry as a living, constantly evolving thing with a great past that we can best cherish by treating it as part of our present. The poems of these exemplars will continue to nourish us for decades to come. Of few predictions can I be so confident.

CHAPTER SIX[25]

2019: "Mischief, thou art afoot."

In *The Unquiet Grave,* his book of *pensées* in the manner of Pascal, Cyril Connolly has a line that in its form may be the prose equivalent of a two-line imagist poem. "Poets arguing about modern poetry: jackals snarling over a dried-up well." Connolly wrote the line in 1945, but you can still hear that snarl today. Ubiquitous instruments of social media make it easy for anyone to pop off, get attention, air grievances, join the mob. While there is little enough criticism in the traditional sense, there is a tremendous amount of rage, and it fuels a censorious impulse that spells trouble for writers, publishers, believers in free speech, and readers of works that get denounced for one reason or another and then get pulled off the shelves.

The mob struck often in 2018. Certain radio stations, bowing to pressure, refused to air "Baby, It's Cold Outside," the classic duet and holiday favorite that won an Academy Award for Frank Loesser in 1949. Recorded by such redoubtable duos as Betty Carter and Ray Charles, Dinah Shore and Buddy Clark, Margaret Whiting and Johnny Mercer, the song is a long goodbye as on a balcony in Verona, only our Romeo begs for five minutes more and Juliet doesn't say yes and she doesn't say no.[26] The preceding sentence alludes to a play and two classic American popular songs for the reason that the predicament of girl fending off beseeching boy at the door is a show-biz tradition.[27] The offense: the song—courtly by the standards of some popular songs today—can be construed not as the clever repartee of a persistent suitor and an ambivalent lady, but as a melodrama in which the villain will stop at nothing to take advantage of the damsel in distress. This is a nutty argument, reminiscent of the inattentive college student who somehow got the idea that "The Rime of the Ancient Mariner" describes a journey to a honey-sweet land of charm and romance.

The distinguished First Amendment attorney Floyd Abrams deplored what he called the "self-abasing decisions" made by important publications.[28] Three such stood out for him. *The New Yorker* invited Trump crony Steve Bannon to take part in a discussion, where you may be quite sure that he would have been raked over the coals by moderator and audience. But the magazine felt compelled to withdraw an invitation, because of Bannon's extreme right-wing views. More grievous was the case of Ian Buruma, who lost his job as editor of the *New York Review of Books*, because he published a mediocre and arguably repellent article by a man with a history of sexual harassment. "Reflections from a Hashtag" by former CBC radio broadcaster Jian Ghomeshi reeked of puffed-up self-pity, but that's not what caused an outrage. What irked people was the very fact that the paper was giving a hearing to the disgraced broadcaster. Staffers grumbled that the decision to publish the piece was made against their wishes. Social media magnified the furor. "Now let it work," Mark Antony said after firing up the crowd in *Julius Caesar*. "Mischief, thou art afoot."

According to Buruma, a cabal of university presses, without whose advertising dollars the paper could not long survive, threatened a boycott. And the magazine that had once instructed readers on how to make a Molotov cocktail—the magazine that prided itself on printing fiery exchanges of in-your-face letters from angry readers and unrepentant writers—fired its top editor, a *New York Review* contributor since 1985. I was "convicted on Twitter," Buruma said.[29]

In midsummer 2018, a poem in the pages of *The Nation* spurred an angry backlash and a craven apology. "How To" by Anders Carlson-Wee used Black English for a monologue from an apparently homeless person asking for a handout. When it transpired that the author was white, a Twitter firestorm erupted in protest of the writer's appropriation of a black person's voice. The criticism, shrill and shaming, had its intended effect. The poetry co-editors of the magazine apologized, as did the author. So much for the tradition of editorial independence. So much for the habit of standing behind what you have published and welcoming letters to the editor in protest or support. Longtime *Nation* columnist Katha Pollitt voiced her dismay on Facebook: "So embarrassing! The poetry editors, Stephanie Burt and Carmen Gimenez Smith, liked the poem enough to publish it, which means they read it many times and did not see problems, but when challenged by the Twitter mob they folded and sent themselves to reeducation camp. Now the whole magazine looks ridiculous. Thanks a lot!"

We who work on *The Best American Poetry* are familiar with such controversies. For all we know, it is possible that something in this edition of *The Best American Poetry* may raise hackles. We don't anticipate that, but even if we did, I like to think that we would stick to our guns as we offer the seventy–five poems that Major Jackson, our editor, has chosen as representative of the best poetry getting written today. I advocate making bold statements, offering no apologies, and leaving it up to others to mount arguments in favor of, or against, poems that are their own best defense.

. . .

Major Jackson is one of the foremost poets of his generation, and a natural choice to make the selections for *The Best American Poetry 2019*.

As we headed into production, I asked Major how the experience affected him. "Most of my free time was spent reading to the 10th power," he said, balancing this activity with work on his own manuscript in progress, *The Absurd Man*. "I'd find myself tinkering on old poems (or yes, starting a new poem) after having imbibed on the verbal richness of others almost like having eaten a can of Popeye's spinach." In his own poems he felt pushed, he added, toward "great pockets of humor, if not a lyricism that hinted at the issues" facing us as a society. To the pessimists among us, Major has a succinct credo: "Poetry, like all art, never goes out of fashion. The will and spirit to represent our inner states and outer truth never dies. Humankind, as historians and scientists have observed, has continually sought new forms to reflect the changing shape of our existence. What waxes and wanes is our willingness to hear each other, to give each other a reading." To do that is exactly the mission of this book.

Pessimism is perennial. In September, the poet Sally Ashton told me of a discovery she made in the stacks of the San Jose State University library: a 1926 anthology of American poetry in thirteen-volumes edited by Edwin Markham, author of "The Man with the Hoe," a poem that achieved great popularity and raised the general awareness of the plight of laborers. Markham began his introduction to the anthology with these sentences that push back against the naysayers:

> Certain critics are saying that poetry is doomed to perish, to be sponged out by the hand of science. As well say that poetry will obliterate science, for each stands on its own ground, separate and secure, coequal, eternal, like Jungfrau and Matterhorn. Others, again, are saying that the world of poetry has been exhausted by the poets themselves—that nothing new is left to see or to say. But these, too, are idle words.

Substitute "technology" for "science" in this formulation and what remains is robust confidence. Do poets today have that confidence? And do people who believe that poetry is "doomed to perish" realize that this prediction is as worn and threadbare as it is?

As the editor of *The Best American Poetry 1989,* Donald Hall addressed these questions in his introduction, which appeared in *Harper's* bearing the headline "Death to the Death of Poetry." It may well be the single best riposte to the bi-annual magazine article predicting the demise of poetry and verse. Lionhearted Don died last year at the age of eighty-nine. He was a mentor and a model for me. A beloved professor at the University of Michigan, he gave up a coveted appointment (with tenure and all its perks) in exchange for a life of jeopardy, "forty joyous years of freelance writing." He made his living by his pen (literally; Don hired someone else to do his typing for him). He wrote about subjects not strictly literary, tried his hand at a variety of genres (children's literature, sports journalism), interviewed eminences, explored other arts (sculpture, painting), edited journals and anthologies, wrote textbooks. Working with him on BAP 1989 was a wonderful experience—in their differing ways, he and John Ashbery taught me more than anyone else about editing a poetry anthology. In 1994, Don asked me to succeed him as the general editor of the University of Michigan Press's Poets on Poetry series. As it was Don who invented the series, he and I were its only editors for its first thirty years. A denizen of New Hampshire, Don loved baseball in general, the Boston Red Sox in particular, so when it was my turn to toast him on the occasion of his seventieth birthday in 1998, I turned to the erstwhile national pastime, recalled that the Dodgers had exactly two managers for four decades, and grandly declared that the two of us were "the Walter Alston and Tommy Lasorda / of the University of Michigan Press, / and though you and I are not exactly like / either of them, Michigan links us / and we have uniform jackets to prove it."

Don won many accolades, book prizes and medals, and was appointed the nation's poet laureate in 2006. "Poetry is my life," he wrote in *Essays after Eighty* (2014)—it was at the vital center of all his activities. He identified himself as a poet even before his student years at Phillips Exeter, Harvard, and Oxford. With his versatility and energy, he always demonstrated the value of hard work in one's poetic practice. The title of *Life Work*, his 1993 memoir, sums up in two words the moral imperative that work represented for Hall. He revised incessantly, always believing that a better draft lay ahead. "Some of these essays took more than eighty drafts," he tells us in *Essays after Eighty*. Provocative, fearless, Hall warned against the "Workshop Poem, McPoem, Clone-Poem, or Standard American Poem" in the 1980s. Aspiring poets who wish to write prose would do well to observe Don's strictures: "Don't begin paragraphs with 'I.'" "Avoid 'me' and 'my' when you can." "Do not commit dead metaphors." "Overuse or misuse of adjectives and adverbs makes prose weak and lethargic." "When we hope to persuade, we should pay court to the opposition."[30] In his essays he wrote what I call exclamation-point sentences, sentences next to which I place an exclamation point in the margin. In "Thank You Thank You," a recent essay in which Don muses about the effect of poetry readings on the composition of verse, note in this sequence of sentences how cogent analysis and historical example give way to whimsy, humor, casual insight, and a totally unexpected opinion:

> Sound had always been my portal to poetry, but in the beginning sound was imagined through the eye. Gradually the out-loud mouth-juice of vowels, or mouth-chunk of consonants, gave body to poems in performances. Dylan Thomas showed the way. Charles Olson said that 'form is never more than an extension of content.' Really, content is only an excuse for oral sex. The most erotic poem in English is *Paradise Lost*.

It's hard to stop reading at this point, isn't it? Don's opinions were exemplary in the sense that they always made you think. And he had generosity of spirit; he felt, as I do, that the warring factions and movements of contemporary poetry can sit down and break bread together.

To the memory of Donald Hall, we dedicate this volume in *The Best American Poetry* series.

CHAPTER SEVEN[31]

2020: "I was once Walt Whitman."

To one who monitors the news for manifestations of poetry in unusual places, 2019 did not disappoint. The cover of the March 25 issue of *Time* featured a picture of an orange peach. The headline: "Do They Dare?" The subhead: "The Democrats will likely impeach." The echo of "The Love Song of J. Alfred Prufrock," the prematurely balding fellow who wonders whether he has the gumption to eat a peach, confirmed something I learned teaching a course called "Great Poems" at New York University: that "Prufrock" remains the modern poem they love best, these talented first-year students who qualified for the college's honors program and enjoyed memorizing sonnets, comparing carpe diem poems by Donne and Marvell, and discussing whether "Kubla Khan" was really a mere fragment, as its author claimed.

On the front page of *The Wall Street Journal* bearing the same date, a tripartite headline observing haiku rules caught my eye: "Haikus About Space / Make Science Less Tedious / So Hope Scientists." Daniella Hernandez's story imparted news of "sciku," the use of the haiku form instead of a one-sentence summary of a study in lunar and planetary science. For example, Aine O'Brien's "The Effects of Shock and Raman Laser Irradiation on the Maturity of Organics in Martian Meteorites" is easier to grasp when summarized in seventeen syllables spread over three lines in units of five, seven, and five syllables: *Look at falling sky / Rock from big red rock in black / Sky to find life signs.* That is quite impressive, and the whole phenomenon adds to evidence I have gathered that the haiku may be the perfect form for an age of shortened attention spans.

In 1986, the Library of Congress rechristened the position of "consultant in poetry" to "poet laureate." Since then, the designation has spread from nation to state, city, county, and borough. In April, the Academy of American Poets announced that thirteen poets laureate will receive a combined sum exceeding one million dollars "to support civic programs." One of the lucky thirteen is the guest editor of this year's *Best American Poetry*. Paisley Rekdal, poet laureate of Utah, plans to sponsor a statewide poetry festival and to launch "Mapping Literary Utah," a website devoted to the work of writers who live or have lived in Utah. Jeanetta Calhoun Mish, poet laureate of Oklahoma, will present poetry workshops in rural areas. Grace Cavalieri of Maryland is lining up newspapers to publish Maryland poets.

Dana Gioia, in his stint as poet laureate of California, visited each county in the state, a feat requiring heroic measures of stamina. Karen Craigo, Missouri's current poet laureate, plans to gather a collection of poems from all of the state's 114 counties. Claudia Castro Luna, poet laureate of the state of Washington, will convene poetry workshops and readings along the entire length of the Columbia River. William Carlos Williams wrote that he was "the happy genius of [his] household," and maybe that's another way of saying the poet laureate of the backyard. The designation does get taken to an incongruous extreme at times. Last August, *Atlanta* magazine broke the story that Waffle House has tapped Georgia Tech professor Karen Head as the chain's first official poet laureate. When asked how a Waffle House is like a poem, Professor Head pointed out that both poetry and hash browns are "made things."

More news of poetry's therapeutic powers surfaced in 2019. In addition to its palliative value, reading or writing poetry "can heal," according to the poet and physician Rafael Campo, who teaches at

Harvard Medical School and works at Beth Israel Deaconess Medical Center in Boston. A pilot study at Northwestern University's medical school aims to ascertain whether "reading poetry with patients has the potential to help alleviate doctor burnout."[32] During the daily "grim half-hour" when the editors of *The New York Times*'s national desk convene daily, the session begins with a poem, somewhat in the way prayers may have served in the past. The poems come from Billy Collins's anthology *Poetry 180*. Marianne Boruch, Langston Hughes, Wordsworth, David Ignatow, Paul Verlaine, and Charles Simic are among the poets whose words read aloud have blessed the editors.[33] It is nevertheless true that *poetry* still shows up sometimes in the old philistine way. A dour *New Yorker* article on that most dour of subjects, Brexit, listed some of the woes that have befallen Great Britain since June 2015:

> [Boris] Johnson asked the Queen to shut down Parliament; the Supreme Court opened it up again. He called for a general election; the Labour Party, led by Jeremy Corbyn, refused to agree to one unless Brexit was delayed. The pound fell. Death threats multiplied. Politicians quoted poetry. A third of British adults said that Brexit had affected their mental health. A man in a clown outfit stood outside the gates of Parliament shouting, 'Save our bendy bananas!'[34]

In that succession of dire sentences, you wonder what "politicians quoted poetry" is doing.

Walt Whitman and Emily Dickinson are the two nineteenth-century American poets who continue to exert the greatest influence on contemporary poetry. In 2019, the bicentennial of Whitman's birth was celebrated with exhibitions devoted to the poet at the New York Public Library, the Morgan Library, and the Grolier Club in New York City. The shows triggered glowing articles about the bard of democracy. In *The New Yorker*, Peter Schjeldahl made the astute observation that "If Keats was 'half in love with easeful death,' Whitman was head over heels for it, as a subject fit for his titanic drive to coax positive value from absolutely everything."[35] In September, the US Postal Service released its 85-cent Walt Whitman stamp covering mail weighing up to three ounces. The Whitman stamp features a portrait of the poet by Sam Weber based on a photograph taken by Frank Pearsall in 1869. A lilac bush and hermit thrush in the background are meant to remind correspondents of Whitman's elegy for Abraham Lincoln, "When Lilacs Last in the Door-yard Bloom'd."

The Library of America published *Walt Whitman Speaks: His Final Thoughts on Life, Writing, Spirituality, and the Promise of America* edited by Brenda Wineapple. (In conversation, Whitman foresaw threats to "free speech, free printing, free assembly," amounting to a "weapon of menace to our future.") Also in 2019, poets made efforts to accord landmark status to Whitman's Brooklyn residence at 99 Ryerson Street. Seeing the house for the first time "brought tears to my eyes," Douglas Crase wrote in a plea to the Landmarks Preservation Commission. "Through that door space in 1855 walked Walt Whitman, at the very time he was about to publish the book that would change American literature forever." The Landmarks Commission has balked because the structure is undistinguished architecturally. Nevertheless, it is the only remaining New York City building that served as the poet's residence. There are shrines to the poet in Huntington, Long Island, where he was born, and in Camden, New Jersey, where he spent his final years. But the place where he lived while finishing and publishing *Leaves of Grass* is unmarked and subject to the considerations of realtors and builders. Shouldn't there be a site in Brooklyn to honor the author of "Crossing Brooklyn Ferry"?

At an international festival at the Walt Whitman Birthplace in August, Robert Schultz delivered a talk on "Walt Whitman and the Civil War," reflecting the work he and Binh Danh have done collaboratively on this important subject. *War Memoranda: Photography,*

Walt Whitman, and Memorials, their book, contains Danh's cyanotypes of Civil War battlefields and Schultz's chlorophyll prints—portraits of Whitman and of Civil War soldiers developed in the flesh of leaves. The conference at the birthplace was moderated by the redoubtable Ed Folsom of the University of Iowa, who chaired no fewer than eight conferences devoted to the "good gray poet" in 2019.

In conjunction with *North American Review,* Brian Clements launched "Every Atom" (as in "every atom belonging to me as good belongs to you"), a series of 200 entries on consecutive days from poets and other Whitman lovers, who were asked to select a passage from Walt and to annotate it, as Martín Espada did on day one (May 31) with reflections on the wonderful lines from "Song of Myself" that begin "Walt Whitman, an American, one of the roughs, a kosmos." It is a happy choice, illustrating "Whitman the visionary, the prophet of the new politics and the new poetics."[36]

On June 11, the poet Richard Jackson quoted these famous lines from "Song of Myself": "Do I contradict myself? / Very well, then . . . I contradict myself. / I am large . . . I contain multitudes." The lines are Whitman's way of saying, with Emerson, that "A foolish consistency is the hobgoblin of little minds, adored by little statesmen and philosophers and divines." There are, Jackson said, dozens of Walt Whitmans afloat. "I was once Walt Whitman," Jorge Luis Borges wrote in "Camden, 1892," and one notes, too, Pessoa's "Salutation to Walt Whitman"; Lorca's "Ode to Walt Whitman" and Neruda's ode with the same title; Hart Crane extending his hand to his forerunner in "The Bridge"; Allen Ginsberg imagining Whitman in a California supermarket; and A. R. Ammons beholding the "radiance" of creation in "The City Limits."

The lines justifying self-contradiction can amount to an anticipatory defense of personae, masks, and heteronyms. On June 22, Julia Alvarez (whose work is included in this year's *Best American Poetry*) picked up the theme, writing that "In his 'Oda a Walt

Whitman,' Neruda claims Whitman taught him to be Americano by celebrating a hemispheric America large enough to include everybody. There was something simpatico—a word Whitman himself uses—between the poet and Hispanic ways of seeing and saying and moving through the world. In fact, when I encountered Jorge Luis Borges's translation of *Leaves of Grass* into Spanish (*Hojas de Hierba*), the poem didn't sound translated—it flowed beautifully in Spanish, as if that had been its origin language."

The celebration of Whitman's bicentennial was complicated by the knowledge that in 1874, Walt denigrated the intellect of black people. Matthew Zapruder in his "Poem for Harm" spoke of his disappointment: "I believed you / your whole life you made // one book some people / now take out into the forest // to ritually burn / because elsewhere you wrote // when you were more than / old enough to know // what you truly thought / of the intellect // of black folks who / were not inside your song."[37] Even as we enshrine Whitman, it is wise to remember that approval of his poetry was never universal—that as he aged, he tended to revise his poems for the worse and that biographical facts or rumors injurious to his reputation surface now and then. Poetry has always been a contested field, and Willa Cather, back in 1896, argued that Whitman's egalitarianism meant the forfeiture of a moral imagination. She wrote that he "accepted the world just as it is and glorified it, the seemly and unseemly, the good and the bad. He had no conception of a difference in people or in things. All men had bodies and were alike to him, one about as good as another. To live was to fulfill all natural laws and impulses. To be comfortable was to be happy. To be happy was the ultimatum. He did not realize the existence of a conscience or a responsibility. He had no more thought of good or evil than the folks in Kipling's Jungle book."

Maybe so, but I would prefer to let Neruda, as translated by Martín Espada, have the last word. Here is the conclusion of "Ode to Walt Whitman":

But
your voice
sings
in the train stations
on the edge of town,
your words
splash
like
dark water
across
the
loading docks
at night,
and your people,
white
and black,
poor
people,
simple
as all people
are simple,
do not forget
your bell:
they congregate singing
beneath
the magnitude
of your spacious life:
they walk among people
with your love
nurturing the pure evolution
of *fraternidad* across the earth.

. . .

I have a natural respect for poets who write prose, can meet deadlines, and undertake ambitious projects. Paisley Rekdal does these things energetically. For her poems she has won the admiration of other estimable poets; her work was selected for five of the last eight volumes of *The Best American Poetry*. Among her books I have a special fondness for *Intimate: An American Family Photo Album*, a memoir dealing with the mixed-race marriage of her parents. The prose is interspersed with the photos of Edward Curtis, who, in Theodore Roosevelt's words, "lived on intimate terms with many different tribes of the mountains and plains." Some of Rekdal's entries are prose poems. One begins: "As a child I was often confused as to who was Chinese and who was white. I thought David Carradine was Chinese. I thought Yul Brynner was Chinese. I thought Tom Brokaw, who looked like my mother's youngest brother, Kingsley, was Chinese. Everyone was potentially Chinese, just as everyone was also potentially white." Paisley worked hard on this volume, never losing her sense of humor. On January 13, she told her Twitter followers. "In the unending series of online distractions to help keep me from finishing this introductory essay to a volume of poetry I edited, I have bought a 2-piece satin suit, an owl house, pendant lights, an ice cream cake, slippers, and now a ukulele." One list of her favorite poems from the year's magazines was headed "Poems I will not cut on pain of death."

At a time when misinformation can spread with Internet speed, it bears repeating that the choices for each volume in *The Best American Poetry* series are made by the guest editor, whose autonomy is guaranteed; the series editor can advise but not insist. Aside from picking the guest editor and assisting her, the series editor attends mainly to the preparation, production, and promotion of the book. It is his job to supervise the process—to write a foreword, to obtain and to edit the guest editor's introduction and the contributors' notes and comments, to enforce such rules as we have (no translations, for example), to acquire permissions, to assemble the manuscript, to help choose the cover art, and to work with the publisher as we rush to meet imminent deadlines.

The Best American Poetry is constantly evolving, not just because of the passage of time—the 2020 volume will necessarily differ from the one dated 1990—but because there is a different guest editor each year. Like a moving object in space, poetry cannot be located with precision, because the tools of measurement affect the outcome. The best we can do is to represent as many legitimate points of view as are commensurate with the size of the nation, the various factions competing for attention, the demographic and regional diversity of our writers, and the rival conceptions of poetic excellence. I may or may not agree with the guest editor's selections, but the whole point of the exercise is to foreground that person's taste, to allow a practitioner of the art to win a readership for the poems that she or he admires the most. This is so whether the criteria are based on personal taste, a political conviction, a sense of some ineffable something that resists definition, a value placed on intelligence, urgency, charm, complexity, emotional resonance, the pleasure principle or principles derived from Arnold, Eliot, Leavis, Ricks, Bloom, Vendler, or one's friends at the AWP convention. Each year's volume may be consulted as a criticism of last year's. No volume is absolutely definitive. A friend once quipped that people love to argue about an anthology; some put it down; but everyone wants to be in it. The effect is magnified by social media. Luckily, many poets shun social media altogether or use it for benign purposes only.

In her introduction to this year's volume, the guest editor revives the venerable tradition of querying the title of the anthology. Back in 1988, John Ashbery anticipated the "best" problem and joked, "Maybe we should call the book 'OK Poems of the Year.'" I often wonder why poets have worried the question while it goes unmentioned in anthologies of the year's best stories and essays. If anyone has a theory, I'd like to hear it. In his introduction to *The Best*

American Poetry 2006, Billy Collins sizes it up this way: "Several past guest editors have felt a need to make apologies for that superlative. In these hypersensitive times when the lighting of a cigarette is regarded as a mortal offense, why be surprised that the notion of ranking poems would be cause for discomfort?"

. . .

In 1998, we published a volume entitled *The Best of the Best American Poetry: 1988-1997*, with selections from the first ten years of the series. The choices were made by Harold Bloom, the Yale University eminence who died last fall at age 89. Bloom was the most famous, most prolific, and most influential literary critic in America from the time he published *The Anxiety of Influence* in 1973. The title of that book has entered our critical vocabulary, as has Bloom's thesis that a "strong" poet must overcome the influence of a powerful precursor. To become himself, Wordsworth had to contend with Milton, for example, while John Ashbery had to endure a wrestling match with Wallace Stevens.

I had met Harold quite by chance six years earlier. In September 1967, as I was about to enter my sophomore year at Columbia, I borrowed my parents' car and, knowing that Yale began its semester a few weeks before we did, drove to New Haven with a friend hoping to sit in on a class. The administrator we approached was kind enough to direct us to a seminar in modern poetry taught by Harold Bloom. It was the first day of the semester, and the professor told the group that only four modern poets were worthy of our attention: William Butler Yeats, D.H. Lawrence, Wallace Stevens, and Hart Crane. This was bold. Everyone else was taking notes, and Bloom glowered and asked me why I wasn't doing so. Instead of answering, I asked what happened to Eliot, Ezra Pound, William Carlos Williams, and Marianne Moore? "They're not central," he said, which was indisputably a maverick position.

In the 1980s, Bloom embarked on the effort of editing hundreds of volumes of critical essays, turning out an introduction for each. "Harold can write an introduction faster than our staffers can turn out jacket copy," Patricia Baldwin, his chief of staff, told me when I visited New Haven in July 1986. At the time, I was writing regularly for *Newsweek*. At *Time* or *Newsweek* in the good old pre-Net days, the hardest thing about writing a six-column piece on a professor of literature was to persuade your senior editor that you can appeal to a general readership that was generally indifferent to academic scholarship. Here I had a brainstorm. I went in and told my editor that Bloom was "the Henry Kissinger of literary criticism" and got the green light.

I reported that Bloom looked like Zero Mostel and sounded like a combination of Oscar Wilde and an Old Testament prophet. For one who rejoiced in the ecstatic vision of a favorite poet, he exuded a certain charming air of gloom. He told me he knew by heart every line of poetry he ever read that he liked. "My dear," he said, "what matters in literature in the end is surely the idiosyncratic, the individual, the flavor or the color of a particular human suffering." Insomnia allowed him to read and reread to his heart's content.

When the poet John Hollander dropped by, and the three of us went out to lunch, I wondered who would prove the bigger talker, for both John and Harold were amazing monologists (and, incidentally, lifelong Yankee fans). No contest; Harold could outtalk anyone. I liked his avuncular salutations: there was "Uncle Archie" (Ammons), "Uncle Ashbery," and "the noble Merrill." *Newsweek* ran my piece under the heading "Let a Hundred Blooms Flower" (international edition) and "Yale's Insomniac Genius."

Harold edited *The Best of the Best American Poetry, 1988-97* with his usual flair—and his usual knack for arousing firestorms of disputation. He included selections from nine of the books but nothing from the 1996 volume, which Adrienne Rich had edited. In his introductory essay, Harold launched an attack on multiculturalism and identity poetry—in which the author's sex, age, ethnic identity, class, and race trump other considerations—and made it plain that Adrienne's sensibility and taste were to blame. When I couldn't persuade Harold to hold his fire, I phoned Adrienne to give her a heads up. She was very gracious. "Don't worry," she said, indicating that she felt it was "an honor" to be thus assailed by Bloom. *The Boston Review* devoted much of an issue to a discussion of Harold's pronouncements. Most of the writers denounced and dissented in vehement terms. I, who do not set out to court controversy but have learned the publishing value of provocation, was relieved when my publisher informed me that the denunciations had helped sell books.

Bloom's energy never flagged, despite two decades of medical woes that would have arrested a lesser person. Harold wrote right up to the end, by longhand when possible. Writing kept him alive. He wrote books, massive tomes in some cases, on Shakespeare, on the American religion, on Genesis (parts of which, he argued, were written by a woman), and on some of his favorite characters, Hamlet, Lear, Cleopatra, Falstaff, Iago.

My last message to Harold was prompted by a reading of his book on *King Lear*. It was on July 21, 2018. "I am reading your book on Lear," I wrote, "and must reaffirm that you are every inch a genius."

. . .

Postscript, April 2020:

I write in self-imposed isolation, belatedly, as this book is well into production. The Corona virus that originated in Wuhan, China, and is spreading with the speed of a medieval plague, has mandated "social distancing," a phrase now commonplace. In Wall Street lingo, we have suffered a fearful "black swan event" that no economic model could have forecast. The shock to our systems of living and of thought has not yet been fully absorbed, but already the stock market has tumbled, main streets look like ghost streets, schools are closed, colleges have sent their students home, the NBA has shut down, "March madness" was canceled, and spring training, too. Even politicians have taken notice. Emergency measures are taking effect. The effort to create an effective vaccine is under way. We can hope that an antidote is in a chemist's test tube even now. Medical scientists are doing their best to "flatten the infection curve"—to limit the spread of this ultra-contagious virus that has already killed many thousands of people and caused whole nations to close down.

Confined to quarters, I have the luxury of thinking about this plague in relation to those in our literature and history—the ten plagues God visited upon the Egyptians in Exodus; the plague Oedipus brought on Thebes when he committed the twin sins of parricide and incest; the bubonic plague that decimated Europe in the fourteenth century. It is possible to regard the current situation allegorically as a punishment we have brought upon ourselves or possibly as a prophecy of geopolitical warfare or even a radical solution to the problem Malthus posed. Whatever else it is, the disaster is also a failure of the imagination inasmuch as we were as unprepared for it as we were at Pearl Harbor on December 7, 1941. The reassuring thing is that we did win the war that we entered on that day.

In the aftermath of the terrorist attack of September 11, 2001, W. H. Auden's "September 1, 1939" gained a new currency. The most famous line of that poem—"We must love one another or die"—was brutalized in an opinion piece in today's *New York Times* (March 19, 2020), which substituted "help" (and "assist") for "love." The more important point is that Auden's poetry endures. Poetry matters. People instinctively turn to poetry during a crisis, for it is then that we become most acutely aware of our need for beauty, wisdom, consolation, charm, and delight. American poets are and will be living through a crisis worse than any in my lifetime, and how they respond to it will prove a fascinating test and challenge.

CHAPTER EIGHT[38]

2021: "I had not thought death had undone so many."

Eleven of the poets who served as guest editors in this series went on to become U.S. poet laureate, or had already achieved the distinction, including this year's editor Tracy K. Smith. Our editors have won Pulitzers, National Book Awards, MacArthur and Guggenheim Fellowships. Two of them were named poetry editor of *The New Yorker*, which continues to be the premier periodical in which to place a poem. But not until this year did one win the most coveted prize of all, the Nobel, which Louise Glück (*BAP 1993*) received in October 2020.

I admire Louise's immediate response to the news, as reported in *Harper's*. Adam Smith, the chief scientific officer of Nobel Media, tried to interview her on the phone. When asked what the Nobel meant to her, Louise said, "I have no idea. My first thought was 'I won't have any friends' because most of my friends are writers." The interviewer persisted. How important is "lived experience"? "Oh, heavens," she said. "It's barely seven o'clock." Smith pressed on. "But it's so much a feature of your own writing?" Louise: "Is the two minutes over?"[39]

In her Nobel acceptance speech, Louise spoke up for the individuality and intimacy of the poetic act; it obeys imperatives that are private and not meant for the grandstand. "In art of the kind to which I was drawn, the voice or judgment of the collective is dangerous," she said. "The precariousness of intimate speech adds to its power and the power of the reader, through whose agency the voice is encouraged in its urgent plea or confidence." She aligned herself with those poets who "do not see reaching many in spatial terms, as in the filled auditorium. They see reaching many temporally, sequentially, many over time, into the future, but in some profound way these readers always come singly, one by one."[40]

Although I have devoted much energy to the project of enlarging the readership for poetry, I tend to agree that poetry is a solitary act, intimate and precarious A poem is "a communication from one who is not the writer to one who is not the reader," Kenneth Koch rather mystically put it, attributing the statement to Paul Valéry. There does seem to be something mystical about the experience of communion with, for example, a poet who died a hundred years ago and wrote in a language you can read only at one remove. Louise Glück's distrust of the collective has never been less popular than it is at present, which makes the Nobel recognition all the more significant. I am happy to note that Louise continues to write and publish poems of note—such as "Night School," which the guest editor chose for *The Best American Poetry 2021*. It was wonderful to have something to celebrate in a year of plague, of anguish and woe without precedent for most of us.

So many died, lost a loved one, lost a job, made a sacrifice, paid a stiff price, or muddled through in a state of maximum uncertainty in 2020. We also went through a stunningly rapid upheaval in consciousness. Though there had been warnings, we were unprepared for a pandemic, perhaps because we have been distracted by such other disasters as forest fires, hurricanes, earthquakes, tsunamis, and the threat of bombs, missiles, terrorist attacks, volcanic eruptions, nuclear plant meltdowns, and the geologic fate of the earth. Covid 19 was a killer the likes of which we had not encountered since the World War II. By the first of March 2021, we had suffered half a million casualties in the United States alone, a shocking number of them in nursing homes. As the disease raged around the world, respecting no man-made borders, Dante's line, echoed by T. S. Eliot in "The Waste Land," came to the fore: "I had not thought death had undone so many."

Overnight, we went into a recession. The unemployment rate climbed to heights not seen since the Depression of the 1930s. In March, the stock market collapsed, with the S & P 500 losing thirty-four per cent of its value in just twenty-two trading sessions. Emergency conditions prevailed. Even after a strong mid-year rebound, the economy contracted 3.5% in 2020, the largest decline since just after World War II.[41] Small stores shut their doors; famous companies sank. Hertz sold its fleet. Brooks Brothers went out of business. Restaurants died: after 157 years, the Cliff House in San Francisco closed its doors for good, as did the 21 Club in NYC. Airline stocks crashed, and conventional energy firms ran out of gas. Worst hit of all were the leisure and hospitality industries and those who work in them.

Not everyone liked the new restrictions imposed to limit the spread of the virus. People were urged, in some cases required, to wear masks in public places and to practice social distancing, with a mandatory six feet separating any two persons. Morale, shaky from the start, broke. Flagrant cases of police abuse sparked nationwide protests. The presidential election campaign upped the ante while lowering the civility index. Social media exacerbated mob impulses. On the federal, state, and local levels, governments faced unprecedented challenges, which they tried to meet with daily press briefings, massive relief and stimulus packages, the distractions of a permanent floating no-holds-barred political tag-team wrestling match, and Operation Warp Speed, a program to hasten the development of an effective vaccine. It seemed almost miraculous that, by late December, vaccines for a disease unknown twelve months earlier had won the approval of the Federal Drug Administration.

A start-up outfit called Moderna was up there with Pfizer, Johnson & Johnson and other major players in developing the treatment in record time.

The way we conduct our lives and our businesses rapidly changed. Satya Nadella, the highly regarded CEO of Microsoft, commented that "We've seen two years' worth of digital transformation in two months . . . in a world of remote everything." To the amazement of market watchers, stocks recovered in record time. The shares of disruptive technology firms, from Tesla to Zoom, were the rage. With so many able to work from home, the question was just how lasting will be the revolution in work habits.

Meanwhile, the gap between rich and poor isn't narrowing, and the suffering of people, whether for medical or economic reasons, will persist no matter how massive a relief package Congress approves. The plague has delivered a devastating blow to so much that we value: theater, dance, orchestral and chamber music, cabarets, clubs. For the people out of work, the people who have had to close their businesses, the people who have lost a family member to the virus, the people who work (or used to work) at airports and hotels, restaurants, theatres, concert halls, and sports arenas—what, I wonder, can I, can any of us, do as poets?

For poets who teach or work at universities, the pandemic will have profound consequences. Some trends have accelerated, and for those of us who love books, not just the contents but the physical object, from cover to colophon, the idea of reading Proust or Henry James on a smartphone remains an incongruity and becomes a more pressing headache.

Many of us kept journals of the plague year. The wisdom of staying at home, restricting my social life and my contact with the world beyond nature, prompted me to renew an old habit and write a poem a day, which I began doing on August 1st. Three months earlier, I had begun to struggle with the old subjects of doubt, chance, and gambling as sometimes an impulse, sometimes an imperative, and sometimes, alas, an addiction. I had never before felt so strongly that writing a poem was a gamble—with odds only somewhat better than that of a message in a bottle tossed into the ocean. Nevertheless, the act of writing a poem a day is one way of pushing back against an out-of-control world in which one's own volition counts for so little, and I keep doing it.

As a native of New York City, I can't help invoking a special prayer for the beleaguered city. I have in mind a paragraph in "Here is New York," a piece E. B. White wrote on assignment for Roger Angell, his editor at *Holiday* magazine, in 1949. "A poem compresses much in a small space and adds music, thus heightening its meaning," White wrote. "The city is like poetry: it compresses all life, all races and breeds, into a small island and adds music and the accompaniment of internal engines. The island of Manhattan is without any doubt the greatest human concentrate on earth, the poem whose magic is comprehensible to millions of permanent residents but whose full meaning will always remain elusive."

. . .

The series editor of *The Best American Poetry* has a multitude of jobs to do, but undoubtedly the most important is selecting the right person to be the year's guest editor—and getting her or him to say yes. The task of selecting seventy-five poems from the plethora of print and electronic magazines in which poems circulate is far from easy, and I am delighted that Tracy K. Smith agreed to take it on. There are personal reasons beyond the obvious literary ones. Between her undergraduate years at Harvard and her appointment as a Stegner Fellow at Stanford, Tracy studied at Columbia, and she was a star student in a graduate seminar I gave in spring 1996. The subject was the New York School of poets, and her expert imitation of a Kenneth Koch poem was so good that I sent it on to Richard Burgin, who published it in his magazine *Boulevard*. So it was and continues to be with particular joy that I have followed the flourishing of Tracy's career. *The Body's Question* (2003) was awarded the Cave Canem prize for the best first book by an African-American poet. *Duende* appeared four years later, and *Life on Mars* (2011) won her a Pulitzer. Smith's most recent book is *Wade in the Water* (2018). She has also written a memoir, *Ordinary Light* (2015).

In June 2017, Tracy became U. S. Poet Laureate. To accompany her on visits to community centers, she compiled an anthology, *American Journal: Fifty Poems for Our Time* (2018), in the hope of reaching readers who have never given poetry a chance. During the pandemic, she was one of four poets who celebrated National Poetry Month (April) by choosing among submissions solicited for *All Things Considered* on NPR.

Above all else, Tracy K. Smith is a distinguished practitioner of the art. Consider her poem "Ash." The title is either ominous or ironic or both. Using a loose, irregular rhyme scheme, and the force of repetition, Smith converts the humble "house" from essential domicile to multiple metaphor:

> Strange house we must keep and fill.
> House that eats and pleads and kills.
> House on legs. House on fire. House infested
> With desire. Haunted house. Lonely house.
> House of trick and suck and shrug.
> *Give-it-to-me* house. *I-need-you-baby* house.
> House whose rooms are pooled with blood.
> House with hands. House of guilt. House
> That other houses built. House of lies
> And pride and bone. House afraid to be alone.
> House like an engine that churns and stalls.
> House with skin and hair for walls.
> House the seasons singe and douse.
> House that believes it is not a house.[42]

If the poem is an architectural wonder that could house us all, its fate and ours can, like the piece of paper on which it was written, go up in smoke and leave only ash behind. My friend Jamie Katz, the writer and jazz aficionado, pinned this poem to his refrigerator door after it appeared in print (in *The New Yorker*, in 2015, and reproduced elsewhere). "I was so struck by this poem," he said, "written in the present tense but freighted with history, mixing memory and desire, guilt and fear, sex and cruelty—such a visceral poem, concrete and direct, with a strong rhythm pushing it forward, which only adds to its urgent and pleading tone. And yes, why 'Ash'? Is this a house that has already burned down but remains alive in obsessive recall, or perhaps a place—real or imagined—that Smith wishes she could obliterate but can't, because her own life is so bound up in it? And who is the 'we' in the first line? Are we all implicated?"

Smith says she is "most interested in the marginal or overshadowed perspectives, the stories that sit outside of or beneath the central American narrative, or the accepted myths of American identity." That editorial philosophy is consistent with an impulse toward inclusiveness, as the contents of this volume confirm. "I know that who I am—a woman, African American, American, born in the late 20th Century and reckoning with life in the early 21st, etc.—has guided me toward the voices, stories, places, possibilities that interest and preoccupy me," Tracy told an interviewer from *Stay Thirsty*.[43] When asked why she chose to express herself in poetry rather than in prose, Tracy answered: "Poetry feels sacred to me, even when it is playful, secular, gritty. Poetry feels like the syntax of the unconscious mind, or—better still—the soul. I love prose, I write in other forms, but I believe that poetry unites me with my largest, perhaps my eternal self."

On January 20, 2021, a day filled with speeches and solemn oaths, the youngest inaugural poet in American history stole the show. Amanda Gorman, 22, who graduated from Harvard in June 2020, boldly and with perfect poise recited her poem "The Hill We Climb." The better verb would be "performed," for Amanda knew the poem as well as an actor knows her lines, and she delivered it with a winning confidence, using hip-hop rhythms and rhyme to excellent effect—commanding the audience rather than retreating from it, as some poets instinctively do. In the poem she read, she pictures herself as "a skinny Black girl / descended from slaves and raised by a single mother," who had (and may still have) a "dream of becoming president." She gave voice to the theme of unity: "We close the divide because we know, to put our future first, / we must first put our differences aside." In a reference to the riots at the Capitol on January 6, she wrote, "while democracy can be periodically delayed, / it can never be permanently defeated." The sentiments were lofty if unoriginal; the rhymes appealed to the ear, and the presentation won listener's hearts.

One day later, Penguin Children's announced that "due to overwhelming demand" it would publish a special hardcover edition of the "The Hill We Climb" with a first printing of 150,000 copies. By the twenty-eighth of January, the publication date was moved up to March 16 and the first printing elevated to one million copies. It was also announced that Oprah Winfrey would write a foreword for the book and that Gorman would write a poem for delivery at the Super Bowl in February. She planned to celebrate the game's three honorary captains: an educator, a nurse manager and a Marine Corps veteran.

The emergence of Amanda Gorman as an overnight sensation was without doubt the poetry event of the year. She didn't exactly come out of nowhere. She introduced Hillary Clinton at the 2017 global leadership awards, was celebrated by Michelle Obama at the White House, and opened for Tracy K. Smith at the Library of Congress. How did all this happen for the Los Angeles native? It goes back to 2017, when she was named America's National Youth Poet Laureate, the first t0 earn that designation. Growing out of programs on the local and state level, the National Youth Poet Laureate was an initiative undertaken by the Urban Word, a New York outfit headed by Michael Cirelli, himself a talented poet and a pedagogic innovator. Influenced by the spoken word movement and the idea that performance and presentation are and should be integral to the creative process, Cirelli believes that literary excellence is compatible with political engagement. "We're still a tiny organization, but we built this huge platform for young poets in their teenage years," he told me with pride and a trace of awe. To identify "the best poets and the ones most invested in social impact," the Urban Word employs a group of judges to choose among four finalists aged fourteen to nineteen, who must submit a poetry portfolio, a CV, a video in which they introduce themselves, and an essay stating what they would do if selected. It is an annual appointment. In 2020, the fourth in the series was named: sixteen-year-old Meera Dasgupta of New York, whose commitment to social change—a requisite—is to the causes of gender equality and climate change. As to the success of the first National Youth Poet Laureate, Cirelli jokes that Amanda Gorman's "bio goes out of date every two weeks," so swift has been her climb, so charismatic her personality, so fierce her energy and determination.

From the start, this anthology series has acted on the belief that many varieties, schools, and movements of poetry can coexist and even flourish in a shared space. I take "unity" in the larger context to mean the same sort of respect and tolerance; the sense, too, that all of us are greater than the sum of our opinions; and the conviction that disagreements, whether literary or political, can be settled peaceably. But better than any definition is an example. During the Civil War, Walt Whitman spent three years visiting wounded soldiers in hospitals in and near Washington, D.C. To the patients he brought gifts to the patient, ministered to them, talked with them, listened. In his new book *The Dharma of Poetry*, the poet John Brehm writes:

> Among the many remarkable aspects of Whitman's wartime service, perhaps most remarkable is this willingness to tend to Confederate as well as Union soldiers, even though his own brother had been wounded at Fredericksburg, and would later nearly die of starvation in a Confederate prison. Whitman's compassion made no distinctions, and that generosity of spirit informs one of his great short lyrics about the war, published in 1865, after the fighting had ended.

Brehm follows with a brief Whitman poem that sublimely illustrates the poet's generosity of soul. The poem is "Reconciliation"

> Word over all, beautiful as the sky!
> Beautiful that war, and all its deeds of carnage, must in time
> be utterly lost;
> That the hands of the sisters Death and Night, incessantly
> softly wash again, and ever again, this soil'd world:
> For my enemy is dead—a man divine as myself is dead;
> I look where he lies, white-faced and still, in the coffin—
> I draw near;
> I bend down, and touch lightly with my lips the white face
> in the coffin.

CHAPTER NINE[44]

2022: "Real life at a social distance."

Years ago, the rumor circulated that secretly it was I who picked the poems for the annual *Best American Poetry*. Perhaps I should have felt flattered. Did I really wield so much power and influence? Did anyone seriously believe that I could dictate to Charles Simic, Adrienne Rich, John Hollander, Rita Dove, Robert Creeley, et al.? On the face of it, the notion was absurd. *The guest editor chooses the poems.* His or her autonomy is guaranteed as a ground condition, and we go to pains to emphasize this fact.

I esteem the poems in this year's *Best American*, not just for their particular virtues, but precisely because they are the picks of Matthew Zapruder, whose knowledge of poetry today makes him an ideal witness. Some of my own favorite poems of the year are in these pages, but some that didn't make the cut deserve acknowledgment, and I would like to draw attention to them here.

Poetry is sometimes newsworthy, as when a "new" poem by a great writer comes to light. In March 2021, London's *Times Literary Supplement* published a 1942 poem by Vladimir Nabokov that previously only a few scholars had read. A lover of Superman, the comic-book hero that a pair of Cleveland lads, Joe Shuster and Jerry Siegel, concocted, Nabokov wrote "The Man of To-morrow's Lament" at the suggestion of his friend Edmund Wilson. Superman, the speaker of the poem, contemplates the dire predicament that threatens his romantic life:

I'm young and bursting with prodigious sap,
and I'm in love like any healthy chap—
and I must throttle my dynamic heart
for marriage would be murder on my part,
an earthquake, wrecking on the night of nights
a woman's life, some palmtrees, all the lights,
the big hotel, a smaller one next door
and half a dozen army trucks—or more.

Even worse would ensue if somehow his romantic partner survived and a "monstrous babe" was born to them. That is why, he tells us, he gets gloomy whenever he "tucks away" the "red-cloaked, blue-hosed" uniform of Superman and dons the coat and trousers of Clark Kent. There's a statue of him in Central Park. But "I stare ahead / and long to be a normal guy instead."

An example of the mock heroic as practiced by such as Alexander Pope in "The Rape of the Lock," Nabokov's bawdy poem—composed by a non-native speaker of English who had only recently arrived in America—is steeped in the conventions of poetry. Scrupulously rhymed, the poem alludes to *King Lear*—Clark Kent is "a banished trunk (like my namesake in 'Lear')"—and makes a knowing aside about Berchtesgaden, the Bavarian Alps retreat favored by Hitler. But the most striking thing about "The Man of To-morrow's Lament" is that Nabokov puts his erudition and sophisticated technique to the service of a bubble-gum fantasy that captured the imagination of young people at the dawn of an era that idealized youth culture. In a sense, the poem is a prelude to the romance of adolescence in Nabokov's most famous novel, *Lolita*. Considered in the light of Pop Art in general and Roy Lichtenstein's paintings in particular, "The Man of To-morrow's Lament" is a prophesy of what took the art world by storm in the 1960s.

In 1942, Nabokov submitted the poem to *The New Yorker*. Charles Pearce, the magazine's poetry editor, rejected it. In addition to the risqué element, he wrote, "Most of us appear to feel that many of our readers wouldn't quite get it."

Two poems I admired deal with technology and the changes it has both undergone and forced upon us during the Covid 19 pandemic. "Zoom Rooms," Mary Jo Salter's sequence of sonnets in the spring 2021 issue of *The American Scholar*, looks at "real life at a social distance." With rhymes and half-rhymes, Salter makes the effort to come to terms with, and maybe even vitalize, the new jargon. She contends with "zoom" itself, "unmute" ("a word I might dispute /even exists, whether verb or adjective"), "gallery view," and generational tags, such as "Boomer," "Millennial," and "Generation C / for coronavirus." The level of wit in "Zoom Rooms" reminds me that John Donne audaciously used a mathematical instrument as a messenger of love. Consider:

> Depending on the scale of your device,
> the size of a single Zoomed-in human soul
> is that of a sonnet: modest and concise.

The poem is, among other things, a self-portrait in a Zoom room:

> Bookcase-prop and real or fake bouquet
> behind you, well-dressed only to the waist
> as if in a casket, top half on display,
> here's another weirdness to be faced:
> you're in the Gallery. You're shown as one
> of your own satellites—as if the sun
> were both a planet and the Copernican
> magnet for all planets.

The word "cloud" has acquired a meaning unanticipated by Wordsworth in "I Wandered Lonely as a Cloud" or the Rolling Stones in "Get Off of My Cloud." Rachel Hadas, who teaches at Rutgers, found herself conducting her course in "Reading Poetry" via Zoom. In "In the Cloud," which enlivened the May 24, 2021 issue of *The New Yorker*, Hadas modifies her doubts with joyous rhymes while thinking out loud about the faces on the computer screen:

> What does this mean to you? I said.
> What does *beautiful* really mean?
> I asked them as I tried to lean
> into the noncommittal screen,
> scanning until my eyes were sore
> for the soul in each black square.
> Were there really people there?
> Did each name hide a secret face
> sheltering somewhere in place,
> some unimaginable space?

Here's how the poem sums up the current state of communal life in virtual space: "Alone together, here we are, / stranded in our shared nowhere."

To enlarge the sphere of poetry, to keep up with the acceleration of change, to incorporate the age's new materials and lexicon is a daunting task, and I applaud Salter and Hadas for tackling it with formidable intelligence. To confront the new with one of poetry's most traditional devices, rhyme, is a daring move.

Old age, its torments and compensations, may not be quite as resistant to verse as high-tech gadgetry, but it is generally neglected or treated in the context of obituary or elegy. Wordsworth, who was unusual in the sympathy he displayed for old men encountered by chance on his walks, wrote: "We Poets in our youth begin in gladness; / But thereof come in the end despondency and madness." Does this sad progress remain the case? Do we pay enough attention to poets who are writing their best work with seventy-seven years on their heads?

If part of the poet's job is to take a difficult condition and render it exactly but with a certain balancing lightheartedness, Terence Winch does so addressing what he has called "old life" in "That

Ship Has Sailed," which was published on-line in *Across the Margin*. The poem consists of two stanzas, the first of which is ebullient in recalling "our" youth in accents recalling Keats's definition of negative capability. What did "we" read?

Keats and Yeats and all the greats
day and night. We got into fights
in pubs. We drank sixteen cups
of coffee every day. We called in sick
and spent the day in mysteries, doubts,
uncertainties.

The much-shorter second section begins with memory loss but ends not with the senior moments you might expect but with glorious ritual and rich metaphor:

We light a candle
to commemorate crossing
the great divide between
the green island of the young
and the songs in our bones
that have come unsung.

A friend introduced me to Teri Ellen Cross Davis's poem "*Bad Girls* Album Cover," which celebrates the sensuality of Donna Summer as depicted "under a / streetlamp's maraschino cherry glow," with wet black ringlets framing "her light brown-sugared face," and "pouting lips"

slick in shiny scarlet gloss, high heel perched on the lamp's base
plunging the slit of her dress back to reveal a black lace stocking

a garter as garnish—so naughty, so beautiful.

Poets are celebrating the erotic. They are also exercising the right to court a comic muse. Angela Ball's "Mississippi State's Football Coach Ponders the Fake People in the Stands" makes merry with the coach's public statement about playing before a crowd of cardboard cutouts:

> It's science fiction meets haunted stadium:
> you're watching the big game, and you can't move,
> let alone cheer or boo. If it's cool,
> and people enjoy it, great, but it's a little
> surreal, the fake people in the stands.
>
> Do the person impersonators have a lottery
> to see who gets the best seats? Some have way better ones,
> those fake people in the stands

Speaking of sports, I had no idea that the late Dan Quisenberry, the relief ace of the Kansas City Royals in the 1980s, wrote poems until Paul Worley, the poetry editor of *North Dakota Quarterly*, published six of them. Three deal directly with baseball and reveal a sensibility that a sports writer would envy. "Time to Quit" is set in San Francisco. The pitcher is trying to warm up, but

> It's a damp wind-off-the-water cold
> and I'm trying to throw sinkers
> into this gale force
> the ball
> a sparrow in a hurricane
> barely makes it.

"The first time I read these I felt like I was sitting down with an old friend I admittedly only knew via the medium of baseball cards, televised games, and my own dollar store imitations of [Quisenberry's distinctive pitching] delivery," Worley says. He is right to characterize the poems as "deep, moving, complicated," the confidences of a man who "used to be famous," as Quisenberry puts it in "Baseball Cards:

I used to be good
they say
we thought you were bigger
I say
I was

If I were the guest editor of this volume, I would also pick something by Matthew Zapruder.

. . .

Twenty-one years ago, at a literary festival organized by James Tate and Dara Wier at the University of Massachusetts, I met Matthew and was immediately taken by his enthusiasm and by the quality of his poems. I have observed him as an instructor at the New School, as the co-director of the Monday night poetry readings series at KGB Bar, and as an editor-at-large of Wave Books. I am not alone in admiring his work. David Wagoner, Denise Duhamel, Natasha Trethewey, and Paisley Rekdal chose poems by Zapruder for the 2009, 2013, 2017, and 2020 editions of this series. Terrance Hayes, in his note about "The Rose Has Teeth," which Mark Doty selected for *BAP 2012*, wrote that his own poem "found its bones after I read Matthew Zapruder's marvelous poem, 'Never to Return,' in the 2009 edition of *The Best American Poetry*."

When I learned that Amy Gerstler, who made the choices for *BAP 2010*, felt as I did about Zapruder's work, I asked her to write about a poem she admired. She responded with dispatch. "The poem 'My Life,' from Matthew Zapruder's 2019 book *Father's Day* is emblematic of what's heart-expanding about his work. Composed predominately of two- and three-word lines with minimal punctuation, the poem is a halting outpouring (if that's not too oxymoronic a phrase), a quiet, unresolved struggle with emotional recalculation and acceptance. 'My Life' is a double origin story, a poem in which the speaker recounts both his son's conception and birth and his own sea change/rebirth as he becomes not just a father but parent of a neurodivergent child. 'My Life' begins with the protagonist and his wife trying to conceive: 'four years ago/on Martin Luther King Day/ in the afternoon/the little strip/said it was time.' The poem progresses through 'the year/of diagnosis when/our life kept/being a place for worsening fears,' to 'then came the proud/sleepless happy/ sorrow months.' As evidenced in these lines, an obsession with time is one of the poem's engines.

"Despite its title it's hard to label 'My Life' confessional because the poem exercises so much discretion, and never loses sight of its own subjectivity. Rather than make that subjectivity a central tenet, as confessional poems from the past often do, 'My Life' keeps doubling back and interrogating itself. The poem's tone of confiding worry is leavened with humor, self-awareness, and a hard-won tenderness that rises through the poem, eventually overtaking, or at least, by the end, running neck and neck with its sadness and fears. Zapruder has a unique ability to ponder contemporary life's specific predicaments (ethical, personal and political) with radical humility and chastened hope."

That I rely on the guest editors I have worked with must be evident from my many references to them in this foreword. Sadly, we lost two in 2021. Robert Bly, who made the selections for *BAP 1999*, died in November. He was 94. It was he who gave me the idea of writing a poem each day, which is what he was doing in January 1996, the coldest January in years at Bennington College. He wrote first thing in the morning, while curtains remained drawn. He would sit up in bed, in close contact with what he called his reptilian brain, and write at a time when travel across the Maginot Line of consciousness went both ways on uncongested highways and took unpredictable turns—not a metaphor Bly would have liked, by the way, not only because he didn't go to history for his rhetoric but also because, dreadful as it was, the world did not face what France faced in May 1940. Robert liked images—a turtle, a spear, an onion, a castle—and wishes, like the desire to travel far or to be in Paris on a Thursday on your last day alive. A big man, the author of "The Teeth Mother Naked at Last" among other arresting titles, he vigorously promoted the prose poem as a form or genre. He advanced his ideas about masculinity in *Iron John: A Book About Men,* a fixture on best-seller lists for more than a year. Robert was said to be cantankerous, but I found him generous, loyal, an excellent teacher and raconteur, and it was a joy to walk with him—and to work with him on *The Best American Poetry 1999.*

On December 18, David Wagoner, the guest editor of *The Best American Poetry 2009,* died in his sleep at the age of ninety-six. When he read for the series, he was, at eighty-two, the oldest of our guest editors, and yet one of the most assiduous in monitoring the landscape and representing the entire range of American poetry. In his introduction to the anthology, David wrote: "Why do people write poems? There are probably a hundred answers to that question, maybe more, but some writers feel they have important messages to give mankind, and of course they usually turn out to be strangely inaudible to that vast audience. Some people just like to play around with words as they might with jigsaw puzzles or pinball machines. Some indulge themselves with poetry secretly, in words as private as diary entries. For some it's a form of public speaking, and they look for audiences in social clubs, or open mics, or even on street corners, making themselves heard to strangers. Some hear their own voices and the voices of other people speaking to them in half sleep and feel obliged to write down what they say in order to understand their own existence more fully. For a number of them, what starts out to be a kind of game turns out to be the most complex and rewarding of all game-like activities, something more nearly religious, as demanding and baffling and compelling as ethics, metaphysics, the search for a god, or even love."

ENDNOTES

1 Other launch readings have taken place at Columbia University, Seton Hall University, the Alliance Française, and elsewhere in New York City through the auspices of the Academy of American Poets, New York University, the Huntington (Long Island) Poetry Festival organized by Faith Lieberman, and the Decatur Literary Festival in Atlanta.

2 The forewords written for *The Best American Poetry* from 1988 through 2014 were collected and published under the title *The State of the Art: A Chronicle of American Poetry, 1988-2014*, by the University of Pittsburgh Press.

3 From the 30th anniversary edition of *The Best American Poetry 1988*, ed. John Ashbery, series ed. David Lehman. Scribner, 2018.

4 David Lehman, Foreword *The Best American Poetry 2015* (Scribner).

5 James Parker, "The Last Rock-Star Poet," *The Atlantic*, December 2014, pp. 50-52.

6 Douglas Belkin, "For College Students, History's a Mystery" *The Wall Street Journal*, October 15, 2014, p. A6.

7 *The American Scholar*, Spring 2013, p. 38; p. 43.

8 Ariel Kaminer, "Accusers and the Accused Crossing Paths at Columbia," *The New York Times*, December 22, 2014, p. 1.

9 "100 coups de fouet, si vous n'etes pas morts de rire!"

10 *Time*, January 19, 2015, p. 62.

11 *The Atlantic*, June 2000.

12 From *The Best American Poetry 2016* (Scribner, 2016).

13 From *The Best American Poetry 2017* (Scribner, 2017)

14 George Orwell, My Country Right or Left (volume two of *The Collected Essays, Journalism, and Letters*), edited by Sonia Orwell and Ian Angus, p. 195, p. 334.

15 "October 1," *The Evening Sun* (Scribner, 2002).

16 Originally in *The Double Dream of Spring* (1970).

17 "The Poet & The City" in *The Dyer's Hand* (1962).

18 I have read a version of this memorable limerick in which "Bolshie" "replaces "great Marxist" in line one and "grand Marxist" in line five.

19 From *The Best American Poetry 2017* (Scribner, 2017).

20 "Can Kevin Young Make Poetry Matter Again?" by Robert P. Baird, *Esquire*, Nov 8, 2017. http://www.esquire.com/entertainment/a13135556/kevin-young-poetry/

21 Robert P. Baird, "Spend It All," Best American Poetry blog, January 12, 2012. http://blog.bestamericanpoetry.com/the_best_american_poetry/2012/01/spend-it-all-by-robert-p-baird.html

22 Shagpat is the tyrant whose power inheres in his hair in George Meredith's novel *The Shaving of Shagpat*. "Rhyme removed, much ethereal music leaps up from the word, music which has chirped unnoticed in the expanse of prose. Any rhyme forbidden, many Shagpats were unwigged." —T. S. Eliot, "Reflections on Vers Libres" (1917).

23 Carl Wilson, "Why Rupi Kaur and Her Peers Are the Most Popular Poets in the World," *The New York Times*, December 15, 2017; Nina Sovich, "My Love Is Like a Hashtag: 'Instagram Poets' Sell Well," *The Wall Street Journal*, September 11, 2017; Priya Khaira-Hanks, "Rupi Kaur: The Inevitable Backlash Against Instagram's Favourite Poet," *The Guardian*, 4 October 2017. The only lines of verse quoted in Nina Sovich's "My Love Is Like a Hashtag" were "Love made / her wild" by Thom Young, apparently a swipe at the pseudonymous Atticus, author of *Love Her Wild* (Atria Books).

24 MedusaSansFrontières@OpheliaInWaders and IanWhittington@Sir__Ian are the Twitter handles.

25 From *The Best American Poetry 2019* (Scribner, 2019).

26 For a more recent interpretation, see the song as performed by Chris Colfer and Darren Criss in the tenth episode of *Glee*'s second season.

27 "Five Minutes More" (Jule Styne and Sammy Cahn); "She Didn't Say Yes, She Didn't Say No" (Jerome Kern and Otto Harbach); the balcony in Verona: *Romeo and Juliet*.

28 Floyd Abrams, *The Wall Street Journal*, Sept 29-30, 2018: "Retreating from, let alone abandoning the intellectual battlefield will only encourage more cries for self-censorship by offended readers. There is simply no excuse for these so often revered publications to comport themselves as if they resided in some sort of cultural re-education camp."

29 Interviewed in *Vrij Nederland*, Buruma said this of the *Review*'s publisher: "No, he did not fire me. But he made clear to me that university publishers, whose advertisements make publication of *The New York Review of Books* partly possible, were threatening a boycott. They are afraid of the reactions on the campuses, where this is an inflammatory topic. Because of this, I feel forced to resign—in fact it is a capitulation to social media and university presses." Conor Friedersdrof, "The Journalistic Implications of Ian Buruma's Resignation," *The Atlantic*, September 25, 2018. See also Lionel Shriver, "Easy Chair," *Harper's*, February 2019, pp. 5-7.

30 The first two of these quotations are from *Essays After Eighty* (Mariner Books), the third from *Breakfast Served Any Time All Day* (Michigan) the final two from the third edition of *Writing Well* (Little, Brown).

31 From *The Best American Poetry 2020* (Scribner, 2020).

32 Sumatha Reddy, "A Prescription of Poetry," in *The Wall Street Journal*, December 2, 2019, p. A11.

33 Marc Lacey, "How Poetry Shakes Up the National Desk's Morning Meetings," *Times Insider*, March 5, 2020.

34 Sam Knight, "The Long Goodbye," *The New Yorker*, November 4, 2019, p. 18.

35 Peter Schjeldahl, "The Song of a Nation," *The New Yorker*, June 24, 2019. pp. 74-75.

36 And I would commend Espada for singling out the passage as it appeared in the 1855 edition of the poem. Whitman weakened the line in later versions: "Walt Whitman, a Kosmos, of Manhattan the son."

37 Matthew Zapruder, *Father's Day* (Copper Canyon Press, 2019).

38 From *The Best American Poetry 2019* (Scribner, 2019).

39 "Prize Fighter," *Harper's* (January 2021), P. 17.

40 https://www.nobelprize.org/prizes/literature/2020/gluck/lecture/

41 Harriet Torry, "US Economy Suffers Worst Year Since '40s," *The Wall Street Journal*, January 29, 2021, p. A1.

42 The poem appeared in *The New Yorker*, November 23, 2015.

43 https://staythirstymagazine.blogspot.com/p/tracy-k-smith-conversation.html

44 From *The Best American Poetry 2022*. Scribner, 2022.

ACKNOWLEDGMENTS

It is a pleasure to acknowledge Scribner, the publisher of *The Best American Poetry* since our inception in 1988, and the University of Pittsburgh Press, which, in *The State of the Art*, published my forewords for the volumes dated from 1988 through 2014. Among the many who have given me good advice, editorial and otherwise, are Mark Bibbins, Elaine Equi, Edward Hirsch, Major Jackson, and Terence Winch. Amy Gerstler and Jamie Katz wrote about particular poems at my request. I am indebted to my literary agents, Glen Hartley and Lynn Chu, and to Sandy McIntosh of Marsh Hawk Press, who believed in this project from the start. Stacey Lehman remains ever and always my first reader.

ABOUT THE AUTHOR

David Lehman launched *The Best American Poetry* in 1988 and continues as the annual anthology's general editor. Educated at Columbia and Cambridge universities, he has written for publications ranging from *Newsweek, The New York Times, The Wall Street Journal,* and *The Washington Post* to *American Heritage, Art in America, Partisan Review,* and *People.* He has taught at Hamilton College, NYU, Bennington, Columbia, and the New School. He edited *The Oxford Book of American Poetry* and is a contributing editor for *The American Scholar.*

Titles From Marsh Hawk Press

Jane Augustine *Arbor Vitae; Krazy; Night Lights; A Woman's Guide to Mountain Climbing*
Tom Beckett *Dipstick (Diptych)*
William Benton *Light on Water*
Sigman Byrd *Under the Wanderer's Star*
Patricia Carlin: *Original Green; Quantum Jitters; Second Nature*
Claudia Carlson *The Elephant House; My Chocolate Sarcophagus; Pocket Park*
Lorna Dee Cervantes: *April on Olymbia*
Meredith Cole *Miniatures*
Jon Curley *Hybrid Moments; Scorch Marks; Remnant Halo*
Joanne D. Dwyer *RASA*
Neil de la Flor *Almost Dorothy; An Elephant's Memory of Blizzards*
Chard deNiord *Sharp Golden Thorn*
Sharon Dolin *Serious Pink*
Joanne Dominique Dwyer *Rasa*
Steve Fellner *Blind Date with Cavafy; The Weary World Rejoices*
Thomas Fink *Zeugma, Selected Poems & Poetic Series; Joyride; Peace Conference; Clarity and Other Poems; After Taxes; Gossip*
Thomas Fink and Maya D. Mason *A Pageant for Every Addiction*
Norman Finkelstein *Inside the Ghost Factory; Passing Over*
Edward Foster *A Looking-Glass for Traytors; The Beginning of Sorrows; Dire Straits; Mahrem: Things Men Should Do for Men; Sewing the Wind; What He Ought to Know*
Paolo Javier *The Feeling is Actual*
Burt Kimmelman *Abandoned Angel; Somehow; Steeple at Sunrise; Zero Point Poiesis; with Fred Caruso The Pond at Cape May Point*
Basil King *Disparate Beasts: Part Two; 77 Beasts; Disparate Beasts; Mirage; The Spoken Word / The Painted Hand from Learning to Draw / A History*
Martha King *Imperfect Fit*
David Lehman: *The Best of* The Best
Phillip Lopate *At the End of the Day*
Mary Mackey *Breaking the Fever; The Jaguars That Prowl Our Dreams; Sugar Zone; Travelers With No Ticket Home; Creativity*
Jason McCall *Dear Hero*
Sandy McIntosh *The After-Death History of My Mother; Between Earth and Sky; Cemetery Chess; Ernesta, in the Style of the Flamenco; Forty-Nine Guaranteed Ways to Escape Death; A Hole In the Ocean; Lesser Lights; Obsessional; Plan B: A Poet's Survivors Manual*
Stephen Paul Miller *Any Lie You Tell Will Be the Truth; The Bee Flies in May; Fort Dad; Skinny Eighth Avenue; There's Only One God and You're Not It*
Daniel Morris *Blue Poles; Bryce Passage; Hit Play; If Not for the Courage*
Gail Newman *Blood Memory*
Geoffrey O'Brien *Where Did Poetry Come From; The Blue Hill*
Sharon Olinka *The Good City*
Christina Olivares *No Map of the Earth Includes Stars*
Justin Petropoulos *Eminent Domain*
Paul Pines *Charlotte Songs; Divine Madness; Gathering Sparks; Last Call at the Tin Palace*
Jacquelyn Pope *Watermark*
George Quasha *Things Done for Themselves*
Karin Randolph *Either She Was*
Rochelle Ratner *Balancing Acts; Ben Casey Days; House and Home*
Michael Rerick *In Ways Impossible to Fold*
Corrine Robins *Facing It; One Thousand Years; Today's Menu*
Eileen R. Tabios *Because I love you I Become War, The Connoisseur of Alleys; I Take Thee, English, for My Beloved; The In(ter)vention of the Hay(na)ku; The Light Sang as It Left Your Eyes; Reproductions of the Empty Flagpole; Sun Stigmata; The Thorn Rosary*
Eileen R. Tabios and j/j hastain *The Relational Elations of Orphaned Algebra*
Tony Trigilio: *Proof Something Happened; Craft: A Memoir*
Susan Terris *Familiar Tense; Ghost of Yesterday; Natural Defenses; On Becoming a Poet* (editor)
Lynne Thompson *Fretwork*
Madeline Tiger *Birds of Sorrow and Joy*
Tana Jean Welch *Latest Volcano*
Harriet Zinnes: *Drawing on the Wall; Light Light or the Curvature of the Earth; New and Selected Poems; Weather is Whether; Whither Nonstopping*

YEAR	AUTHOR	TITLE	JUDGE
2004	Jacquelyn Pope	*Watermark*	Marie Ponsot
2005	Sigman Byrd	*Under the Wanderer's Star*	Gerald Stern
2006	Steve Fellner	*Blind Date with Cavafy*	Denise Duhamel
2007	Karin Randolph	*Either She Was*	David Shapiro
2008	Michael Rerick	*In Ways Impossible to Fold*	Thylias Moss
2009	Neil de la Flor	*Almost Dorothy*	Forrest Gander
2010	Justin Petropoulos	*Eminent Domain*	Anne Waldman
2011	Meredith Cole	*Miniatures*	Alicia Ostriker
2012	Jason McCall	*Dear Hero,*	Cornelius Eady
2013	Tom Beckett	*Dipstick (Diptych)*	Charles Bernstein
2014	Christina Olivares	*No Map of the Earth Includes Stars*	Brenda Hillman
2015	Tana Jean Welch	*Latest Volcano*	Stephanie Strickland
2016	Robert Gibb	*After*	Mark Doty
2017	Geoffrey O'Brien	*The Blue Hill*	Meena Alexander
2018	Lynne Thompson	*Fretwork*	Jane Hirshfield
2019	Gail Newman	*Blood Memory*	Marge Piercy
2020	Tony Trigilio	*Proof Something Happened*	Susan Howe
2021	Joanne D. Dwyer	*Rasa*	David Lehman
2022	Brian Cochran	*Translation Zone*	John Yau
2023	Liane Strauss	*The Flaws in the Story*	Mary Jo Bang